DATE DUE

~~MAY 12 1994~~		~~JUL 15 2002~~	
	~~APR 21 1994~~		
~~OCT 31 1994~~			
~~NOV 14 1994~~			
		DEC 11 2014	
~~JUL 2 1995~~			
~~4-15-96~~			
DEC 18 2004			
DEC 11 2014			
W/D			

Demco, Inc. 38-293

MUSIC THERAPY IN
CHILD PSYCHOSIS

MUSIC THERAPY IN CHILD PSYCHOSIS

By

ROLANDO O. BENENZON, M.D.

Translated from the original Spanish
Musicoterapia en la Psicosis Infantil

By

Wanda Grabia

With a Foreword by

Asher Bar, Ph.D.

CHARLES C THOMAS • PUBLISHER
Springfield • Illinois • U.S.A.

Published and Distributed Throughout the World by

CHARLES C THOMAS · PUBLISHER
2600 South First Street
Springfield, Illinois 62717 U.S.A.

© 1982 *by* CHARLES C THOMAS · PUBLISHER
ISBN 0-398-04646-8
Library of Congress Catalog Card Number: 81-21373

Printed in the United States of America

I-R-1

Library of Congress Cataloging in Publication Data

Benenzon, Rolando O.
   [Musicoterapia en la psicosis infantil.
English]
   Music therapy in child psychosis.

   Bibliography: p.
   Includes index.
   1. Music therapy. 2. Psychoses in children. I. Title.
[DNLM: 1. Music therapy--In infancy and childhood.
2. Psychotic disorders--In infancy and childhood.
3. Psychotic disorders--Therapy. WS 350.2 B465m]
ML3920.B413 1982   618.92'891654   81-21373
ISBN 0-398-04646-8   .   AACR2

To my mother

FOREWORD

ONE OF THE MORE EVIDENT PROBLEMS that affect psychotic children in general, and autistic children in particular, is the breaking of verbal communication with their environment. This situation has led many professionals and nonprofessionals to say that autistic and psychotic children are incapable of communicating and overcoming the marked backwardness observed in their evolution, which is very rarely completed. As a result, traditionally, psychotic children were neglected as soon as any attempt to teach them verbal communication failed.

Dr. Benenzon's brilliant and innovative contribution to the understanding of nonverbal communication with psychotic children has no precedents in the literature published to date on the subject. He recognizes that psychotic children communicate using nonverbal means and that verbal communication can be established on nonverbal foundations.

An autistic child's refusal to communicate verbally is an act through which he communicates his "rejection." The child expresses his unwillingness by nonverbal means. When an autistic child reacts to a musical stimulus by bodily movements, isolated sounds, emission of sounds, words, or dancing, he is displaying a possibility of communication.

Verbal communication appears as the final objective of a series of communicative acts, which may start with a movement of the eyes, smiles, screams, or other nonverbal actions. When the sound of water or music produces such actions, they become appropriate therapeutic stimuli for nonverbal communication.

For these children, communication through nonverbal action should become the prerequisite for verbal communication.

Professor Benenzon's work brings out these points clearly, both in theory and in practice. His work with psychotic children has a special quality. It is the study of a pioneer, capable of contributing relevant theoretical foundations for his clinical experiments and of producing excellent results.

ASHER BAR
Head, Department of Communication and Audiology Pathology
Otorhinolaryngology Service
Mount Sinai School of Medicine
New York, New York

INTRODUCTION

MY ORIGINAL IDEA WAS to describe an approach methodology and technique that was developed at the Instituto de Nivelación Pedagógica in Buenos Aires with children suffering from serious behavior and personality disorders and whose traits form the broad picture of child psychoses. However, I have added a synthesis of music therapy principles and methodology as well, since they have had to be adapted to be used in child psychosis.

The approach techniques I am referring to use sound fundamentally in the broadest meaning of the term, and their objectives create an opening towards other therapeutic techniques: recovery, relearning, or rehabilitation.

I consider that sound is capable of crossing barriers unsurmountable to visual, tactile, and other stimuli. This concept derives from the peculiarity of the sound stimulus which makes it different from any other, and whose characteristics we shall analyze in this book.

The great world of sound which surrounds us is still therapeutically unexplored and unexploited. This is also true of the counterindications related to possibilities of communication. When I speak of the world of sound, I refer to silence, movement, bodily sounds, natural sounds, and those of musical instruments, of electronic devices, etc. Therefore, we may mention heartbeats, white noise, a sinusoidal sound, or a fragment of Mozart's Fortieth Symphony. I shall place these techniques in the field of music therapy; that is why I must explain what I understand by the term.

Music therapy is an auxilliary of medicine, (it therefore belongs to the paramedical disciplines) which deals with the application of any sound element, whether musical or not, in order to produce regressive states and open channels of communication for the relearning process and the recovery of the individual for society.

The term *music therapy* is certainly not adjusted to the concept of this specialty, but we accept it because it is traditional and because we do not have any other which could cover the meaning of nonverbal theory and training for nonverbal thought and communication. The term *music therapy* does not fill today either the requirements or the real objectives of this branch of science. One of the reasons for this is the importance of the different parameters that compose the sound structure and which can also be found in the complicated rhythmical, melodic, and harmonic structures of what we call music.

What may be really useful, for therapeutical purposes, may be only one given parameter. Under these circumstances, it is possible that a Stravinsky symphony will provoke a given mobilization of our dynamic psyche, but this mobilization may depend on intensity, timbre, density, etc., of the music, or perhaps only one parametric aspect played by the bassoon may be of importance.

Some authors prefer to call it "therapy through sound."

Finally, I want to refer to one of the most sensitive subjects in the field of music therapy: that of the training of the music therapist, his personality, and learning characteristics. Since music therapy is a communication technique that uses sound, music, and movement as intermediary objects, and since these preverbal and nonverbal elements make it possible to bring communication back to very regressive states (which enables us to engender a relearning of the patient), it is clear that the music therapist must prepare himself to face his patient's regressive nuclei, some of which are very deep. These nuclei may even mobilize the music therapist's regressive nuclei, which, if he is not well aware of them, may harm communication and the therapeutic objective.

The music therapist must prepare himself so that his thinking can develop at a preverbal level; he must think in sounds, and movements, not words or symbols. He must acquire medical, psychological, and musical knowledge, and yet he must be neither physician, psychologist, nor musician.

He must not be a psychologist, because the latter's training forms him to think, elaborate, and interpret in words or in symbols. Our experience shows that when a psychologist who has musical knowledge as well practices music therapy, he cannot escape his role and tries to interpret psychic dynamics. The music therapist, on the other hand, *acts* the same dynamics in a nonverbal form. For example, a patient begins to strike a cymbal exaggeratedly before a music therapy group; that is clear evidence at that moment, of a reactive formation to the feeling of impotence and need of leadership. A psychologist will interpret the impotence; the music therapist will begin following the patient's complementary ISO, imitating the same intensity of percussion, then leading on to a change of rhythmical intensity which will integrate the patient in the group and strengthen the Ego and the possibility of elaborating the impotence in other terms. The psychologist is accustomed to mobilizing his mind and stilling his body; the music therapist learns to mobilize his body and his mind, synchronizing the sound of his movement to them.

I said that the music therapist must not be a musician. In this case, I refer to the gifted, erudite musician by vocation, whose objective is to interpret, because in his training and in himself he will be educationally and musically prejudiced and this will prevent him from accepting his patient's dissonance or will cause him to reject the lack of rhythm of one patient, the peculiar rhythm of another, etc. I do not include in this aspect the composer, who is usually better prepared for this type of adaptation.

On the other hand, it is frequently observed that the musician who specializes in music therapy becomes frustrated because the main objective of music therapy is therapy and not music.

These observations do not mean that the music therapist should not have musical training; on the contrary, he must have it, but it must be centered on learning the free improvisation and constant creation techniques.

I believe that the music therapist should discover his own ISO, i.e. his own rhythm-sound-music traits, his own sound identity. To this end, it is necessary for each music therapist to go through his own experience of music therapy, during which he will become a patient so that he can recognize clearly his own limitations and characteristics and not confuse them later with those of his patients; he must differentiate what belongs to him from what belongs to his patient.

Finally, I said that he should not be a physician because his function is first to indicate or counterindicate treatment with music therapy and establish its objectives, and second to control and supervise the work of this ancillary to medicine.

In summary, a music therapist must be only a music therapist and must be specially trained to be one. It is the only way to be disconnected from those who distort the specialty, such as certain music teachers who believe that by teaching music to psychotics or patients with cerebral palsy they are practicing specialized musical education. They can do a great deal of good, but their work should not be confused with a therapeutic process.

That is why a music therapist must have optimum mental health. Should a music therapist go through his own psychotherapeutic experience? I think so. A music therapist will face very regressive, clearly psychotic nuclei, which may only appear during a session and which may mobilize some of the music therapist's unconscious nuclei.

Our experience indicates that treatment with music therapy produces a pronounced symbiosis between the patient and the music therapist which recalls the mother-child relationship. That is why we have created some techniques for the termination of treatment to avoid complicated abandonment situations.

The preceding example shows a reason why the music therapist must have his own mother-child conflicts clear. To add weight to this, it must be considered that the history of all great musicians, in fact of all musicians, shows a search for the evocation of the mother-child relationship through music.

In this introduction I have taken the liberty of defining the limits and roles of the therapist because the cases I shall describe cover practically all the fields of music therapy and because I am firmly convinced of its therapeutic properties. For this very reason, I dedicate this book to all graduate music therapists whose training and work I have had the opportunity of directing and supervising — of the Paramedical Disciplines School of the Medical School of the Salvador University in Buenos Aires, Argentina, the Brazilian Conservatory of Rio de Janeiro, Brazil, of the Associação de Musicoterapia do Paraná, Brazil; and the future graduates of the Associação Paulista de Musicoterapia, of the Associação Sul Brasileira de Musicoterapia, Porto Alegre, Brazil, of the Uruguayan Music Therapy Association, the Portuguese Music Therapy Association, and the Association de Recherches et d'Application des Techniques Psychomusicales in Paris, France. My thanks and acknowledgment to them all.

ACKNOWLEDGMENTS

I WISH to thank Angela García Ramírez, educational psychologist, a graduate of Argentine Catholic University and Director of the Instituto de Nivelación Pedagógica in Buenos Aires, for having allowed me to carry out my work at the Institute she directs and for having accepted my request to write Chapter 5 of this book. First, because she gave me the necessary elements and above all a container, i.e. the institution, for these problem children, which facilitated the success of music therapy as a technique integrated to other techniques in a health team, proving in this way that for psychotic, autistic, and symbiotic children, music therapy is the first approach technique towards recovery, and the possibility of other means of rehabilitation. Second, because she has written a wonderful chapter in which she describes the institution in which the experience took place and the philosophy that has made it possible to create and continue working in this type of institution for problem children.

I also wish to thank María Alfonsín de Surmani, music therapist, graduate of the School of Paramedical Disciplines of the Medical School of the Salvador University in Buenos Aires, for her valuable collaboration as a music therapist in the family groups, for having allowed me to supervise individual cases, and finally, for having accepted my invitation to draft the Appendix on music therapy treatment in which she describes the treatment of a blind child with serious behavioral disorders and his evolution as an individual and in the family group.

Finally, I wish to thank María Elena Puzzio, phonoaudiologist, graduate of the Salvador University in Buenos Aires and supervisor of the Department of emotionally disturbed children, for her collaboration in the role of surrogate mother during the first stage of my work and for her intelligent evaluation of the

behavior of problem children as compared with their daily attitudes at the institute.

CONTENTS

Page

Foreword, Asher Bar vii

Introduction. ix

Part 1. BASES AND TECHNIQUES

Chapter

  1. Methodology and Techniques of Music Therapy 5

  2. Symptomatology of Problem Children — Reference Schema 8

  3. Fetal Psyche and Child Psychosis 12

  4. Experiment with Electronic Sounds .15

  5. Helping Children with Emotional Disorders

     Angela Garcia Ramirez. 18

Part 2. MUSIC THERAPY PRACTICE

  6. Music Therapy as a First Approach Technique — Theory. 29

  7. Description of the Music Therapy Session 33

  8. Results of Regression and Communication Levels 38

  9. Communication Cysts — First Approach to the Family Group 45

 10. Effects of the First Approach to the Family Group — Changes

    in the Message. 52

 11. Music Therapy and the Family Group: The Therapeutic

    Couple — Level of Integration 57

Appendix: Music Therapeutical Treatment of a Blind Child with

      Serious Behavior Disorders

      Maria Rosa Alfonsin de Surmani 68

Bibliography. 91

Index 93

MUSIC THERAPY IN
CHILD PSYCHOSIS

Part 1

BASES AND TECHNIQUES

Chapter 1

METHODOLOGY AND TECHNIQUES OF MUSIC THERAPY

OUR METHODOLOGY IN MUSIC THERAPY consists of two parts. The first is of a diagnostic nature and the second is therapeutic. In the diagnostic part, the objective is to discover the patient's or the group's ISO principle and the instrument or instruments that will serve as intermediary objects. ISO means "the same," and in music therapy it consists of the search for the sound identity of the individual by means of which it is possible to achieve nonverbal communication.

The ISO principle is based on the notion of the existence of an internal sound that is characteristic of each of us and individualizes us, a sound that is the sum total of our sound archtypes, our intrauterine and gestational sound experiences, and our sound experiences from birth and infancy up to the present moment. It is a sound structured within a sound mosaic, which is, in turn, built up over time and which is in perpetual movement. In simpler terms, the ISO principle can be described by saying that to produce a communication channel between the patient and the therapist, the mental tempo of the patient must coincide with the sound-music tempo played by the therapist.

If a patient has manic characteristics and, in consequence, has a scattered, quick, accelerated mental tempo, the sound-music tempo must coincide and be quick, *allegro*, *vivace*, etc. Otherwise, it will meet with indifference or rejection.

The ISO may be gestalt, complementary, or group. The gestalt ISO is the mosaic described above, which characterizes the individual; the complementary ISOs are the small changes that occur every day or during each session, caused by environmental and dynamic circumstances. The group ISO is intimately related to the social context in which the individual is integrated. The group ISO requires a certain time to be established and built up. It will often depend on the correct choice of the group and the music therapist's knowledge of the individual ISOs of each patient.

Some people speak of the human body as a resonance box, but I want to make it clear that this is not related to the ISO principle; although entering into resonance with a patient may make communication easier, it may also make it more difficult.

Resonance may be physical or psychic. An example with electronic music may make this aspect clear. There are given low, semi-low, and high electronic sounds which cause the vibration of intestinal, cardiac, and cerebral zones, respectively, independently of any psychological situation. On the other hand, there are other electronic sounds that produce individual memories or mnemonic associations in each patient.

We said that another diagnostic objective is the search for an intermediary object. An intermediary object is a communication instrument capable of acting therapeutically on the patient without setting off states of intense alarm. In psychodrama, for example, puppets are used as intermediary objects. In music therapy, the intermediary objects are the instrument used and the sounds emitted.

We must establish the difference between a puppet as an intermediary object and a musical instrument; in the former, the source of sound will be the psychodramatist, while in the latter case, the sound emission is peculiar and characteristic of the instrument. That is why the intermediary object in music therapy is related to the patient's ISO, and a correct choice of instrument will depend on the skill of the music therapist to discover the patient's sound identity. To discover the ISO and the intermediary objects of a patient, a music therapy questionnaire is drawn up and the nonverbal context is tested.

The music therapy questionnaire is an examination of the patient and/or the parents and grandparents to discover the sound prototypes and the social and environmental elements during the gestation period, all infantile sound experiences and the current ones.

The testing of the nonverbal context consists of placing the patient before a series of simple percussion instruments and a few melodic ones and observing how he manages to use them for communication. This test will show which instrument will serve as an intermediary object and will also verify the hypothesis about the patient's ISO.

The second part is constituted by the music therapy sessions, during which the patient and the music therapist work actively. It is a matter of establishing communication channels at the regressive level by means of the patient's sound identity, and new channels for his future integration in groups or other therapies.

More details about methodology and techniques in music therapy are given in the Music Therapy Manual (*Music Therapy in Psychiatry*, written in collaboration with Antonio Yepes).

Chapter 2

SYMPTOMATOLOGY OF PROBLEM CHILDREN — REFERENCE SCHEMA

IN VIEW OF THE CONFUSION EXISTING on the subjects of child autism, child psychosis, symbiosis, child schizophrenia, etc., I shall try to describe the symptoms of the children we have treated directly, without labelling them with given nosographies.

The first characteristic of these children is that they do not present notable physical disabilities, with the exception of some neurological maturative retardation such as no sphincter control, a certain lack of balance when walking, and some bizarre motor manifestations. In general, they have normal complementary neurological tests, electroencephalographs, amino acid content, arteriographies and tomography.

We may say, therefore, that there is no gross brain damage. However, we do not discard the possibility that in some of these children there may be a minimal brain damage which may complicate or partially cause serious psychological disorders. Many of the symptoms are the same as those described by Kanner, as child autism.

When we observe these cases, we find the following symptoms:

(a) According to Margaret Mahler, they do not establish differences between their parents and strangers. In the presence of their mother, these children have symptoms that show a desperate effort to avoid the catastrophic anxiety that separation from her would produce. Consequently, in her presence they stick to her, and the mother is the only object of communication. Yet, when

8

they are alone, they behave in the same way as autistic children.

(b) They have a remarkable ability to handle objects with which they have a very special affective relationship. These objects are inanimate. E. Rodrigué calls them predictable objects in contrast to the live object, particularly the man-object.

(c) They appear physically intelligent, in contrast to the cretin or the mentally deficient.

(d) Their language has an individual, particular, and strange symbolism; in some cases there is total mutism that brings to mind a deaf child.

(e) Some have an early and agile motor development; on the other hand, others hit themselves on the head and have different manifestations of self-aggression.

(f) In general, they have an exceptional memory.

(g) Some are unsociable and disobedient, which is characteristic of the autistic child; on the other hand, others show adherent behavior and strong tendency to mold themselves like dough to adults, a characteristic Rimland observes in schizophrenic children.

(h) As to the hallucinations some authors think possible in schizophrenic children, we can only refer to attitudes that give the impression of a response to certain hallucinations, above all of the auditory type. This rich symptomatology responds to infinite dynamic processes.

Our experience with these children enables me to distinguish two types of defense, or rather of communication-blocking structures.

One of them – which is more characteristic of the autistic child – is that the Ego is enclosed in a sort of crystal box (Fig. 1). A comparison has even been made with the typical Japanese dolls which meet in their crystal boxes.

The crystal box separates the Ego (doll) from the outside world, and it apparently does not receive any impression from the environment. Under observation, it would seem that the Ego of this child undergoes important dynamic phenomena, but when we try to come closer to the belief that we are going to connect, we suddenly crash into the defensive crystal structure of this child. I consider that this uniform structure belongs essentially to the Ego of this child.

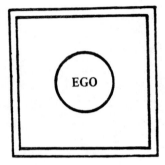

Figure 1. Structure of the autistic child.

In the second— which is characteristic of the symbiotic child — it is only possible to observe the difference in the presence of the mother. When both are present, a massive opening of the crystal structure is observed, through which emerges a pseudopodic prolongation of the child's Ego, which leans against the mother's but does not manage to connect because the mother has already formed a microscopic defensive structure similar to her child's crystal box (Fig. 2). If the mother is not present, the symbiotic child is exactly like the autistic one.

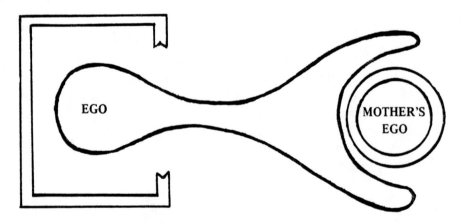

Figure 2. Structure of the symbiotic child.

Finally, we have the structures of those children who are called schizophrenic. In their case, the crystal structure is formed differently. The Ego of the schizophrenic child is divided, and each part is enclosed in a crystal block. Each of these blocks is independent and acts according to the characteristics of the Ego it encloses. The free Ego zones, which are the ones appearing between the blocks, have defenses similar to those of neurotics and together produce a series of bizarre behavior (Fig. 3).

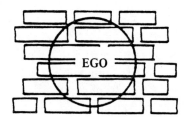

Figure 3. Structure of the schizophrenic child.

The structures described are not totally limited. Children are often observed to have several of them. Consequently, we have children with serious communication disorders which prevent any approach to undertaking recovery therapies. That is why we have tried to discover approach techniques that make it possible to open communication channels to be used by other recovery techniques such as occupational therapy, psychomotor therapy, learning, etc.

The use of sound in all its implications is the basic element of these approach techniques.

Chapter 3

FETAL PSYCHE AND CHILD PSYCHOSIS

BEFORE DESCRIBING OUR EXPERIENCE, I must clarify my concept that "child psychosis, particularly the one that is included in what is called child autism, is a pathological and deformed prolongation of the fetal psyche."

In the light of our current knowledge, it is certain that the fetus responds to internal and external stimuli. The stimuli and the responses to them impress the fetal psyche and create dynamic, mnemonic engrams. This leads to the hypothesis of experience, which consists of the discovery of these mnemonic engrams and using them to open the communication channels of the psychotic child.

In nearly all the gestation histories of children with autistic traits, we find a mother with serious emotional disorders during pregnancy, such as anxiety, anguish, or rejection from the first months. Some even have the typical fantasies of the future symptomatology of the child, such as "I felt that my child was going to be deaf." This is correlated to other studies, such as those made by Sontag, which show that great anxiety in the mother provokes an increase in the motor activity of the fetus.

Severe emotional states during the last months of pregnancy produce hyperactive children who function badly and inadequately. On the other hand, hyperkinetic fetuses later show apprehension patterns in situations with other children at the age of two or three.

For our work, it is interesting to consider more in detail

12

stimuli, sound, and movement during the gestation period. I will quote from my book *Music Therapy Manual* and make some additional remarks to stress the importance of these gestation phenomena.

From the moment that the ovum is joined to the spermatozoon and implants in the mother's womb to develop into the new being, the latter is in contact with the pulsations of the heartbeat and other vibratory sensations of movement and sound resulting from noises made by the uterine wall, by the sound of the mother's breathing, as well as by the different positions due to gravitation.

As the fetus develops, it acquires the sensation of the introjection of this blood pulsation in all its body, associating it with the phenomenon of life, as any changes give it sensations of lack of oxygen, nutrition, thermal regulation, or of a whole called life.

Any alteration in the blood supply or any of its elements through the umbilical cord will cause states of stress or fetal alarm, i.e. an increase of the instinct of life or death. This is related to the heartbeats, which drive the blood flow from the mother to the fetus, but it is also related to other sounds such as that of the breathing of the mother, which may come before or together with the heartbeat, or even vocal phenomena, which will reach it in a distorted form.

Sontag and Wallace provoked alarm responses in a 9-month-old fetus in 28 out of 29 attempts, using an electric bell that tapped (during 5 seconds at 1 minute intervals) a wooden disk placed on the mother's abdomen. A significant increase in the heart rate was noted.

Spelt reported that he managed to condition fetuses. His procedure consisted in 5 second tactile stimuli of the mother's abdomen in the fetal region, followed by a loud noise. This was produced by a small wooden stick beating on a wooden box. After repeated efforts, the fetus learned to expect the sound after the tactile stimulus.

Tomatis assumes that the fetus perceives specific sounds of the mother. Among these sounds, he considers that those corresponding to the voice are of importance for future communication. So, for the treatment of dyslexias and other disorders, he uses the mother's voice heard through filters that gives the sensation of being transmitted through an aqueous medium.

He found that children who are made to listen to the recordings of the mother's distorted voice recognize the words of their own mother and make them intelligible but fail to recognize the voice of other mothers. This can be tested by each one of us. If we listen to any tape after it has been transmitted through a filter, we will not recognize, even after hours of listening, one word pronounced by other women, but if they are the words of our own mother, we will understand more and more words until, in time, we understand everything recorded on the tape.

It is possible that Tomatis' experiments also show us the presence of a massive perception by the fetus of the infinite number of stimuli that reach it. It is certain that the perception does not occur through an auditory or tactile system but as a unit of single sensory perception, as an undifferentiated whole whose essential stimuli are sound-movement. The discovery of these stimuli would be a valuable contribution to the treatment of psychotic patients.

For some years, I was specifically interested in the heartbeat and made a number of experiments, using them for therapeutic ends. In all cases, it appeared that the heartbeat induced in the patients and other subjects regressive and pleasurable situations to a much higher degree than music.[1]

Today, in the light of experience with psychotic children, I consider that (a) the sounds of breathing, (b) the sonority of the mother's voice, and (c) the mother's internal reactions to these stimuli during pregnancy are very important, but may also be a contraindication for communication.

---

[1] These experiments are described in the section on the psychology of sound in Chapter 2 of *Music Therapy Manual* by the same author.

Chapter 4

EXPERIMENT WITH ELECTRONIC SOUNDS

ELECTRONIC SOUNDS have also been used in the work I will describe in the following chapters. Some years ago we started an experiment in the Di Tella Institute electronic music laboratory in order to investigate the psychological effects of electronic sounds. We formed a group of seven physicians working in psychiatry, some of them with training in psychodrama.

The first stage consisted of transmitting, from the laboratory to the acoustic room where we were, pure electronic sounds, such as sinusoidal sound, during 60 minutes. At another session white sound would be transmitted, and so on, successively. At the end of the 60 minutes, we collected on a tape the impressions and free associations produced in each one of us by these sounds.

After a time, this changed to the transmission of definite messages from the composer and sound engineer, and the perception, on our part, of these messages. For example, if the composer wanted to provoke sensations of disgust, sadness, anxiety, or laughter, he was always able to achieve this without difficulty.

In general, these sessions, which took place at 2 PM, provoked intense regressive sensations, which were difficult to rid oneself of during the rest of the day.

There were sounds that produced exclusively somatic components and others that induced a significant psychological involvement. Highly organized material with a tendency to musical content produced intellectual phenomena; on the other hand, constant, continuous material in the same register produced physical phenomena. Among the clearly differentiated somatic zones affected were the intestines, the heart, and the brain, according to whether the sound was low, semi-low, or high, respectively.

Continuous sound gave a sensation of solitude, while pulsations stimulated union and the impression that we were in a group.

Some pulsations were followed by prolonged silences which produced the patellar reflex in the majority.

We easily entered atemporality phenomena. For example, we believed that 10 minutes had gone by when actually it was 25. Among the sensations that the composer managed to produce in the group were claustrophobia, panic, persecution, disgust, nausea, and amusement. All these phenomena existed beyond the purely psychological phenomena of each one of us. That is why I consider that electronic sounds may, by themselves, break well-structured defense mechanisms and can be aptly applied in the obsessive type of disorders.

When the composer, carried away by his musical prejudice, wanted to suggest elements of a purely musical type, they immediately produced an interruption, a differentiation that was noted by all of us.

At the individual level, there were sounds that caused the intercepting of thought or some association in one of us but not in the others.

Should we ask ourselves at this point, going back to the ISO principle, if our internal sound, this characteristic sound that identifies us, could be changed into a characteropathic sound? Or whether this internal sound would, in fact, remain unchanged as a unit belonging to each one of us? Among the therapeutic aspects that emerged from this experiment, we may sum up four that could form part of future research in music therapy:

1. The use of sounds producing exclusively somatic sensations in hypochondriac patients.
2. The use of sounds that intercept thought in some states of delirium.
3. Replacing some hallucinogenic drugs with sounds that produce intense regressive and hallucinatory states.
4. The use of sounds as an approach technique with psychotic

children, as I shall describe in the following chapters.

Finally, the presence of electronic sounds in this work is due to the following:

a. Electronic sound makes research easier, as it enables us to know exactly the parameter of the sound heard and therefore to reproduce it at will.

b. It enables us to find parameters that coincide with those of other sounds of a natural type or with a complicated musical structure.

c. The easy handling of electronic sound makes it possible to change any of the parameters at will, whether intensity, volume, density, timbre, etc., which gives us more scope for research.

d. The experiment mentioned leads us to believe that electronic sound has its own characteristics, which produce different phenomena, including the power to provoke the appearance of very regressive manifestations.

Chapter 5

HELPING CHILDREN WITH EMOTIONAL DISORDERS

ANGELA GARCÍA RAMÍREZ

W HEN DR. BENENZON ASKED US TO DESCRIBE the structure and dynamics of the Instituto de Nivelación Psicoeda-
gógica for his new book, and our experience with a group of autistic children, we felt that it was a heavy responsibility.

It is not easy to speak of

- Ten years of a tremendous human effort.
- A whole attitude to work made up of love and understanding
  for the child and his deficiencies.
- A coherent and systematized multidisciplinary therapeutic
  context.
- A team which, with its advanced techniques, dedication,
  optimism, and patience, contributed to the improvement of
  results.
- And, in particular, the specific atmosphere to be found at the
  Instituto de Nivelación Pedagógica, the atmosphere of ac-
  ceptance, humility, and respect that each one of us finds in
  his interaction with the others.

Though it is not easy, we shall try to do it.

We have been training children with communication disorders
and learning difficulties since 1964. The majority suffered from

Angela García Ramírez is Director of the Instituto de Nivelación Pedagógica, Buenos
Aires, Argentina.

neurological problems and emotional maladjustment.

Until April, 1968, we were prepared for an adequate approach to the problem and had obtained good results. But since then, we had to change our operational strategy. This occurred when a neurologist sent us a child with a diagnosis of aphasia who disconnected us from the start. That child, whom we shall call R.P., was strangely, almost magically, beautiful, sad, and empty, but with some intelligence in his attitude.

His isolation and the tremendous difficulties we had in communicating with him during three months made us think that we had to change our therapeutic approach and try other forms of connecting with him.

It was Arminda Aberastury who showed us the way and told us about a strange mental illness called early childhood autism. She also told us about the best ways to penetrate this secret and ritualistic universe, in which the difference between subject and object is meaningless (Bettelheim) and in which autistic children remain, deprived of any affective contact with the external world.

Our starting point was to set up a total therapeutic habitat around the living enigma that was R.P. and to train him systematically in areas of daily life, since these could also serve as a nexus to relate him to us. This would allow, further on, for adequate mobilization of his affective interactions to enable him to come out of the egocentric level in which he was enclosed both in thought and in action.

The first, message that we sent him was, "We don't ask you anything; we simply want you to feel accepted and comfortable during the time you spend with us." In the first place, we put R.P. in a clean, gay, and comfortable room with enough space for him to be able to move freely if he liked, and by the side of a bathroom which offered the same conditions of comfort and hygiene. We thought that a favorable environment might produce deep and positive changes in him.

This exemplifies the whole attitude of the Instituto de Nivelación Pedagógica: everything that is dirtied or disordered is cleaned and tidied up as soon as possible; everything that is broken is immediately repaired. We cannot submit these children to a dirty, broken, or chaotic habitat; their internal conflict is enough. Two points which are of special importance at the Institute, were

Figure 4. Lunch in small groups with the therapist.

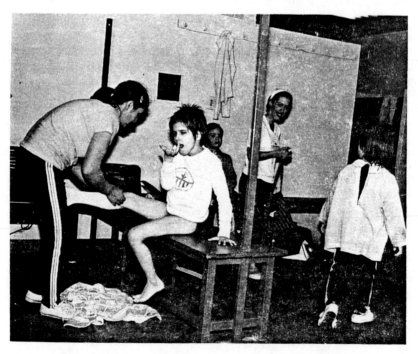

Figure 5. Dressing and undressing to go to the swimming pool.

Figure 6. Integration into groups.

Figure 7. Feeling safe.

Figure 8. Individual body-to-body work.

carefully considered in R.P.'s program of activities: hygiene and nutrition. We felt that a dirty and malnourished child would find it impossible to give and to receive.

It is for this reason that the cleaning personnel (maids and nannies) are helped and directed by our team. This is done considering especially their endless task of cleaning rooms and bathrooms and changing several times a day children who are incontinent, which sorely tries their patience and requires special effort and dedication, particularly as they do not have the gratification proper to a therapist of following and seeing the evolution of a case.

To continue with R.P.: he constantly had a therapist by his side whose most important function was to serve as a depository or container for R.P. and as a mother figure, as well as to be a model for identification at a second stage. Technical perfection, enthusiasm, creative activity, ductility, spontaneity, amiability, persuasion, and a capacity to put limits to critical situations were the necessary traits of this therapist.

The greatest possibilities of contact occured during R.P.'s bath. It was after a long bath that, reinforced by relaxing and pleasurable cutaneous sensations, for the first time he looked the therapist in the face. After a time, we also realized that music offered greater possibilities than other things, and we began to sing him the orders and expressions that we wanted him to fix, but R.P. did not learn any word before the fourth year of treatment.

The responses that we did obtain caused us to open the following year a music therapy department and later a hydrotherapy department, which enabled us to build valuable bridges to come closer to the deep solitude of the autistic child.

As for R.P., during the first months, apart from isolated reactions at bath time or when he was listening to music, we did not achieve any positive relationship with him. Actually, the only times when we felt him to be a person was when he wet himself. It was as if the only thing he could do was to let himself go and let the urine run along his body, his legs, and his trousers while he remained motionless and without any reaction.

After five months, R.P. was still completely centered in himself or, in appearance, molded to his therapist when the latter held him on her lap. Then he looked like an inert part of the adult body and not a child sitting on her lap. The remainder of the time, the fact that he did not use his body and his inert state gave the impression that he had lost interest in the world, that he could not or did not want to take interest in those parts of the body which were precisely in contact with the world.

When he was dressed or undressed, he let himself be moved as if he were a stuffed doll. This suggests that he had also isolated himself completely from his own body. What happened to his body did not happen to him. Nothing that came into contact with him made any connection with what could consititute his inner self. This was true not only of his sense of touch and the movements of his body; we had the same strong impression when, apart from being mute, he seemed blind and deaf, when images and sounds did not produce any reaction. It seemed as if they did not penetrate to him.

SYMBOLIC EXPRESSION

Little by little, parallel acquisitions started appearing in the symbolic behavior, including words, such as would have procured for him a desirable object (a ball, a string of beads). Also, during the individual sessions, he was better able to ask for help, not with words but by singing the song "Give me one hand — give me the other." He began using words to express emotion or affects.

Games

Sometimes his activities with objects extended to people. From parallel games (to other children) he progressed to games requiring interaction. The first and only game we managed to interest him in for a long time was playing ball. Like the very small child, he could only do this with the mother figures, his therapists. In this case, too, there was a long introduction to rotation before he could make up his mind to enjoy throwing the ball weakly when it rolled towards him and then pushing it.

He showed great anxiety and doubts in all this, which revealed how much he feared any active handling of objects and personal interaction. He was still so disconnected from his own body and normal movements that he never seemed to be totally sure that a movement would be effective to solve problems such as returning the ball.

After three years at the Institute, R.P. became increasingly a person, more aggressive, more interested in the world surrounding him. However, he spent most of the time in his isolated retreat, concentrated on his internal bodily sensations and given up to hallucinations and dreams of a more or less stereotyped and limited content, as revealed by his own comments when he answered our questions. The concept of "I" was fully developed, although it was not stable for a time. For example, he said "I" and "I am" excitedly and often as if needing to reaffirm his recently conquered identity to himself.

As occurs with all autistic children, R.P.'s difficulties with pronouns were related to his struggle to separate himself from his world. Even now, when faced with serious emotional problems, R.P. does not use "I" referring to himself but "you," another aspect of the relation between the use of the personal pronoun and the development of the self.

In four years, R.P. progressed to the point of speaking with other children and interacting on his own initiative in his experience of shared scholarship. This naturally made his companions take more interest in him. In fact, some tried to become friends because they thought he responded to their efforts. They no longer found his games and behavior so strange, and they even understood his feelings and what he acted. They reacted with sympathy and tried to help him to solve his problems.

We noted certain intellectual progress, which was much better than his evolution in the freeing of his emotions. After some months of reading easy phrases, he learned to write in capital letters. For this he used material that is closely related to fecal matter: plastilline. The first words he wrote were the same he first learned to read: his own name and the word "ball."

After four and a half years at the Institute, he had learned the rudiments of reading and writing. It was not easy for him to read and write, but he devoted himself to these tasks and made real efforts to understand. It was evident that he was thinking of what he was doing and that he did not try to escape as he did before. When he achieved good results, his face would express great satisfaction. He also progressed in the understanding of his difficulties and his desire to improve and get well. But he often became completely discouraged with himself and told us he was not sure whether he wanted to become an intelligent child or remain as he was. He distinguished clearly between an R.P. who was "mad" and an intelligent R.P. who could write his name.

During the fifth year at our Institute, R.P. worked hard to build himself a better life. He realized that "to get better made you feel worse." and when we asked him what was going worse, he answered "Me." If we asked him more directly "Don't you feel better if you speak of what makes you afraid?", he answered "No, it makes me feel more afraid." In sum, the more he became connected, the more he realized his limitations.

His reading capacity was that of a slow child. He acquired more and more things, but very slowly. This level should have satisfied us, since R.P. had only been with us six years and had begun from scratch. Our disappointment was the greater, however, when we realized that his intellectual progress did not follow his sensory and affective progress. From this point of view, his history is similar to that of some of our mute autistic children; those who spoke developed very differently. It seems possible, certainly to give back an affective life to a mute autistic child, to get him to use all his libidinal energy, but we cannot say the same about his understanding the reality of his Ego.

By dint of love, patience, and understanding, R.P. learned and reached a state in which it was possible for him to live outside a specialized institution, in an ordinary school, and with a socialization that was now offered to him.

Today, R.P. can carry out simple tasks, knows how to look after his person, and can even be useful at home. He looks after his school things and his clothes; he very much likes going to an ordinary school, the camps the school organizes, and his friends' and companions' birthday parties.

What is essential is that this child came to us completely blocked, without the least reaction or response to external stimuli, isolated and vegetative, and that now he is prepared for love and work (Freud).

Our daily task at the Instituto de Nivelación Pedagógica is hard and exhausting; it is a constant challenge in which every minute is precious, but, insofar as we are successful, it possesses the enriching factors of any creation. To take a child out of his enclosure and isolation, this death situation in which he is submerged, and to begin to connect him, to make him communicate, is to teach him to live, and it is a work of art.

Part 2

MUSIC THERAPY PRACTICE

Chapter 6

MUSIC THERAPY AS A FIRST APPROACH
TECHNIQUE — THEORY

THE BASIC OBJECTIVE was to find an approach technique with the children described, starting with the assumption that music therapy is one of the first or priority approach techniques with this type of patient. Chapter 5 explained that music therapy is integrated with other paramedical therapeutic techniques , though in this case, music therapy was the starting point for the opening of communication channels that made possible the use of other techniques or the work of the personnel dedicated to daily life.

Our experience consists of three stages or levels:

1. Regressive level. During this first stage, the patient is exposed to sounds that are empathic to his regressive state and there occurs an opening of channels and a concomitant rupture of defensive nuclei. At this level, passive or receptive music therapy techniques are used.

Passive music therapy is understood to be exposing of the patient to sounds without giving him any instructions first. The case of autistic or psychotic children is the only case in which we can speak of passive music therapy. In all other cases, although the patient is exposed to sounds, he is active, responding in some way to the sound he perceives.

2. Communication level. During this second stage, the patient communicates with the music therapist, who takes advantage of the communication channels opened at the first level to introduce himself as a human being.

3. Integration level. During this third stage, the patient communicates with the environment and with the family group. The channels opened at previous levels are also used.

At the regressive level there are three initial steps, which are shown in Figure 9. The first step (1) is to find the specific sound that can penetrate through the crystal armor to eliminate the Ego of the problem child. In other words, it is to find that child's ISO.

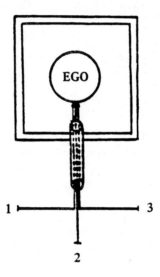

Figure 9. (1) sound; (2) Instrument; (3) Animated source, object-man.

The second step (2) is the introduction of an instrument that will reproduce the sound that penetrated the crystal layer and made an impact on the Ego of the problem child or, if this is not possible, to reproduce some parameter of that sound, which converts the instrument into an intermediary object.

The third step (3) is the appearance of the animated source, the object-man, the music therapist, who, by means of the intermediary object, the instrument, establishes a direct contact with the problem child.

I use the words *direct contact* to establish the difference between this step and the first, during which the music therapist is also present but unable to communicate directly with the child. The third step brings us to the level of communication.

In Figure 10 we can see the fourth step (4), which is the response of the problem child's Ego, which occurs at the same time as the second step (2). This response also opens a communication channel, crossing the crystal armor but inversely to the previous channels, i.e. from the inside out.

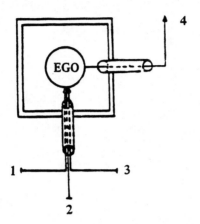

Figure 10. (1) Sound; (2) Instrument; (3) Animated source, object-man; (4) Response (movement, gesture, water games).

This enables us to discover and use a new communication channel, as can bee seen in Figure 11, which is the imitation of the child's response (5). The imitation may be an emitted sound, gestures, or even movements as such.

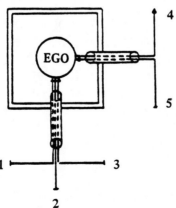

Figure 11. (1) Sound; (2) Instrument; (3) Animated source, object-man; (4) Response (movement, gesture, water games); (5) Imitation (stimulation with water games).

One of the most complicated steps of this process is step (1), i.e. looking for the ISO of the problem child. It is difficult because we cannot use any of the elements of the methodology created for treatment in music therapy. We cannot ask a psychotic child about his sound-music history, that is, using the music therapy questionnaire. Second, we cannot test him as to his non-verbal context, as we would not get any answer. Drawing up the music therapy questionnaire with the parents of these children is a sterile task, since, in general, as we shall see in the following chapters, these parents have a well-defined character structure and it is consequently very difficult to discover new elements in the abundant but rigid history that they give us at the beginning.

This led me to try sounds empirically and intuitively, using above all very primitive sounds with a strong regressive tendency, on the basis that the psyche of a psychotic child, particularly the one with strong autistic traits, is a pathological prolongation of the fetal psyche. So the sounds chosen were those with which the fetus was presumably in contact during the nine months of gestation, such as the heartbeat, intestinal sounds, the sounds of breathing, the sounds made by the uterine wall and the internal voice of the mother, or those external sounds that reach the fetus, filtered by the aqueous medium.

Another problem to be solved was to provide the child with some element with which he could emit a response. This gave rise to the idea of using water. The reasons for choosing water were the following:

1. Water is a common element with which the problem child is in daily contact.

2. It has regressive and gratifying features, i.e. it continues like sounds, establishing a similar situation to the intrauterine one, which in this case would be the amniotic liquid.

3. We have not seen any child reject water except one who associated it with washing his head and cried when he saw water. He changed his attitude completely at the second session.

4. It gives the child the possibility of responding nonverbally by playing with the water.

5. It has special characteristics as an intermediary object. For example, with those children with whom it was· impossible to make skin-to-skin contact because of the child's immediate rejection of the least attempt to touch or caress it, the skin-water-skin contact was achieved in the water.

6. This occurred at the same time as successful practice was started in the swimming pool, as described in Chapter 5.

Chapter 7

DESCRIPTION OF THE
MUSIC THERAPY SESSION

T HE SESSION ALWAYS TOOK place in a different room to the one the child normally used at the Institute. The room used to interview the parents was chosen. This was called the blue room, as the armchairs, carpet, and lampshades are a turquoise blue. This room gives the sensation of being in a home and not in a specialized institution (Fig. 12).

Figure 12.

The decoration was never modified, so that all the variables remained the same except sound, which was the only element to change.

Every session a small desk was put in, and also a chair, which was the same as the one used in the workroom. A round metal dish was placed on the desk and on each side of it a blue, transparent plastic jug full of water. The dish was round and made of metal because this enabled the problem child to emit a sound by tapping his fingers and making the dish turn with a gentle pressure (see Figs. 12 through 15).

The specialized teacher, the surrogate mother of the Institute, sat on one side of the table, and I sat on the other. The surrogate mother was well known to the children, as she spent most of her day with them, and I was only known to some of them. Towels on our laps protected us from violent movements of water.

The recorder was placed on another armchair, but during later sessions it was put on the floor where it was not so visible, as it drew the attention of some children when it was on the armchair, particularly the circular movement of the tapes, as can be seen in Figure 13.

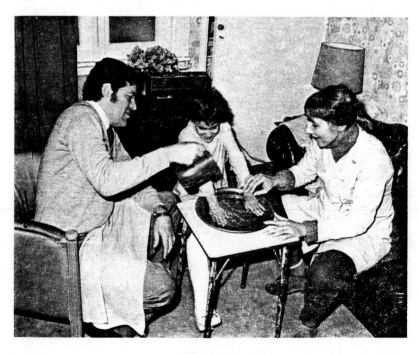

Figure 13.

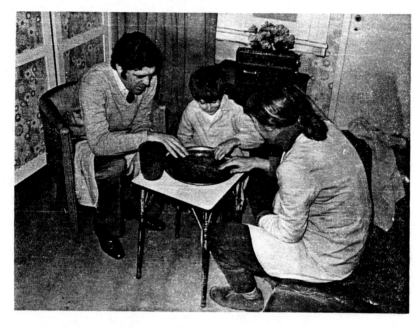

Figure 14.

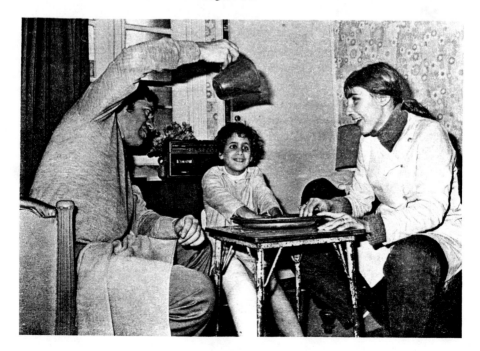

Figure 15.

During the first step, that is in the search for the sound which will make an impact on the problem child's Ego, we work individually during fifteen minutes, two or three times a week. During the fifteen minutes of the session, three sound fragments are emitted, which last five minutes each.

The following are some examples of recorded and emitted sessions.

First session: Five minutes of sinusoidal sound; five minutes of a fragment from Mozart's Fortieth Symphony; finally, five more minutes of sinusoidal sound. That is to say that during all the sessions the last five minutes are a repetition of the first five.

Second session: Five minutes of clicks made with the mouth, of sounds produced by passing tongue over the gums and the strong grinding of molars, and swallowing sounds. All these were obtained by imitating the sounds made by one of the problem children. Five minutes of heartbeat, adding in breathing sounds from time to time, and finally, the sounds emitted during the first five minutes.

Third session: The sounds of breathing through the mouth and the nose; then five minutes of a Brazilian batucada; then the repetition of the first five minutes.

Fourth session: Five minutes of the sound of water drops and a jet of water in a glass that is filling; then five minutes from a song by Harry Belafonte; and again the first five minutes.

The problem child was brought by the teacher (surrogate mother). She encouraged him to start the recorder or did it in front of the child when he could not do it alone. Then she seated him in the little chair in front of the desk and the dish. I was sitting on one side of the desk and the teacher was sitting on the other.

Neither of us said a word or made any sound during the session. The only sound elements, therefore, were the ones coming from the recorder and those which penetrated from outside.

Our attitude during the fifteen minutes of uninterrupted audition was to observe the spontaneous reactions of the child. From time to time, we would pour water into the dish in the sight of the child, and we encouraged him to make ripples or bubbles in the water. If the child put his hands in the water, we tried to caress them in the water or we poured water over them.

After fifteen minutes' audition, we waited in silence for a while, and then the child was taken away by the hand by the teacher. In this way we hoped to find some sound that would make an impact on the child and would produce some characteristic and different response in him.

As soon as a sound is discovered, the music therapist starts working directly. He will introduce some instrument that emits the same sound or some parameter of it, and he will start to work actively with the child. We have reached then the second step of the first level, which imperceptibly leads us to the second level of communication.

The music therapist will try to establish a direct link between the instrument and his person. For this third step, he will not only use the instrument or his own body as an instrument, but also movement, gestures, etc., which are often an imitation of the child's responses.

When the music therapist uses his own body as an instrument, as in the case of his voice, the palms of his hands, heel tapping, clicking, whistling, we cannot speak of an intermediary object as such, as these do not meet the required conditions.

Chapter 8

RESULTS OF REGRESSION AND
COMMUNICATION LEVELS

IN THIS CHAPTER I SHALL FIRST GIVE some general con-
clusions of this stage of the experiment, then some interesting observations of the different cases, and finally, the description
of what happened to a little girl whom we shall call Mary and a
boy we shall call Peter, which will be the two cases whose evolution we shall follow at other levels.

SOME CONCLUSIONS

Experience has taught us to make a differential diagnosis between the child with pure autistic traits and the child with psychotic traits of the schizophrenic type. It became evident that the
autistic child did not respond to any change in the sound stimuli,
particularly during the first and the second five minutes of the
sessions and the following ones, in spite of the contrast between
the examples. The child with psychotic or organic traits, however,
nearly always showed some sort of reaction by making different
movements or gestures, or by emitting different sounds at the
point when the change occurred. The purely autistic child only
responded clearly when we discovered the specific sound that
made an impact on his Ego.

We often observed the difficulty these children have to stay in
one position for a period of time; many of them, for example,
tend to lie on the floor or to assume strange positions. In our experience, except for a very few cases, we managed to get the children to remain seated during the fifteen or twenty minutes of the

session, without trying to move from the chair.

The sinusoidal sound produced calm and sedation in the majority of the children, making it possibile to play spontaneously with the water. There was a suprising case of a little girl who rejected every contact with her hands, hiding them behind her chair or making abrupt rejection movements every time we tried to take them, either to bring them close to the water or to caress them. Yet from the beginning of the sinusoidal session we got her to accept contact and the caress in the water without difficulty, playing in the water and feeling pleasure every time the little jets of water were poured on her fingers (Figs. 16 and 17).

Figure 16.

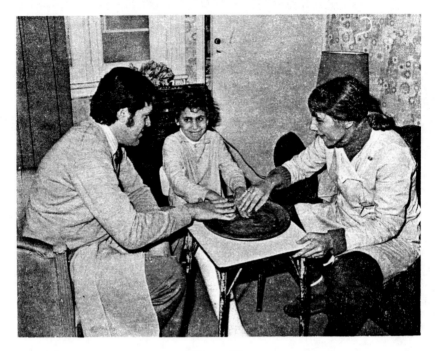

Figure 17.

One of the children, who did not respond to any of the changes of sound and whose only form of exteriorization was clicks and the grinding of teeth, stopped his emission of sounds and listened attentively only when he heard his own clicks recorded.

It was possible to work with the sound of clicking and imitations of it with this child. Other children, whose impacting sound could not be found, maintained stereotyped behavior such as splashing the water, meaningless smiles, eyes vaguely going round the room, turning the dish indefinitely, etc. All these attitudes did not change, even when a technician of the Institute would sometimes come in.

On the other hand, some children with strongly schizophrenic traits, constantly changed their attitudes when they heard a change in the sound coming from the recorder. They stopped their game, waited for a few minutes, listening, and then took up their game again, or stood up to watch the recorder, or were distracted by some outside sound. Another child poured the water from one jug to the other without stopping during the whole session, an attitude that did not change until we found the sound that made an impact on him.

However, the response was different when the sound that was characteristic of his identity was found, that is, his ISO. His reaction was definitive when by modifying and playing with variables of that sound identity it was possible to maintain and continue communication with that child.

MARY'S CASE

Mary came for the first session and passively accepted the pressure on her fingers to start the recorder. She was sitting on the little chair while the sinusoidal sound was being played. Her eyes were absent; her hands were placed in the water. They remained passively in the water, her position being almost catatonic. This attitude was typical of Mary during the other activities of the Institute.

When the fragments from Mozart's Fortieth Symphony started, her attitude remained the same, and only on some occasions there was a passing stereotyped, meaningless smile on her face.

These attitudes did not change during the other sessions. The discovery occurred during the session when the heartbeat, interrupted by breathing, was heard. The change was notable: in the first place, she fixed her eyes (Fig. 18).

This attitude was repeated every time she heard the sounds of breathing. Then she began to imitate these sounds, sighing deeply and becoming very anxious. The first step of the experiment was accomplished.

We repeated the sound with the same results. The music therapist was informed, and he began to work with the sounds of breathing. To achieve the second step, we had to find the instrument that would serve as an intermediary object.

Mary responded quickly to the sound of breathing either imitating or using a different tempo. In the end, the recorder flute was found to be a useful instrument to imitate these sounds and even to get Mary to begin to blow and emit sounds.

Every day Mary communicated more openly with the music

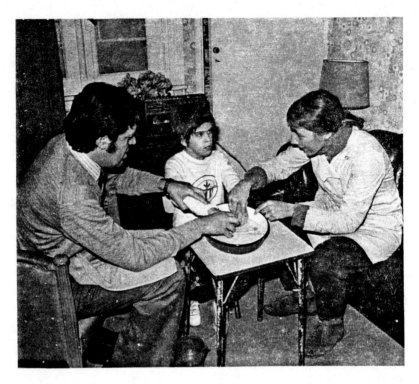

Figure 18.

therapist, who began the task of integrating other elements to the session, such as songs, various tunes, and physical games, which Mary imitated and did obediently. From time to time, she would say some word like "Hello" or the name of the music therapist.

PETER'S CASE

Peter was one of the more difficult children to enter the Institute. There was a constant rejection or a complete indifference when we tried to come close to him. He had no sphincter control, exhibited marked photophobia, and rejected food. He only ingested some liquid or semisolid foods. He was immediately included in our therapy in order to find some point of approach.

When he came to the first session, he started to cry excitedly, hindering any approach to the place of work and tending to lie on the floor. He calmed down when he heard the sinusoidal sound, and he made circular movements of the head in silence without any exteriorization. He did not change his attitude when he heard the Mozart fragment.

Yet, during the second session, when he heard the clicks and then the heartbeats followed by the clicks, he was more amenable to the place of work. Only during the second audition of the clicks could we see an insinuation of movement and an emission of clicks by Peter. We repeated the session and tried to add our own sounds of clicks, with positive results.

We successfully tried eating in the same place. We had achieved the first step.

Figure 19.

Figure 20.

Chapter 9

COMMUNICATION CYSTS —
FIRST APPROACH TO THE FAMILY GROUP

I THINK it is a fundamental rule for the recovery of any child with psychotic traits to work simultaneously with the family. We must modify the family group as we open new communication channels with the problem child, adapting the family to the new channels.

In its daily life with the problem child, the family group created stereotyped communication systems, which hardened over time, forming what I would call real "communication cysts." We shall not discuss whether these communication cysts are the cause or the effect of the psychosis of the child.

We have worked with the child and his family group after they came to us for observation. In general, the parents of psychotic children, and particularly those who have frankly autistic symptoms, usually have characteristic traits. Some are of a high intellectual level and many are professionals. Because of this, when they come to consult us, they present us with an apparently very complete clinical and psychological case history, full of details about all the symptoms, the date of appearance, tests made, and medical examinations.

At first, when faced with this type of history, it would appear that there is nothing more to ask; yet, over time, it is noted that these histories are rigid and unchangeable, becoming very often defenses of very deep information it is impossible to discover. This is one of the reasons why it is difficult to know some aspects of the ISO of these children, as I have mentioned in the first chapters.

Some particulars about experiences during pregnancy, birth, and first days of life are hidden behind the symptomatology observed. We have found that many events that occurred during pregnancy have implications in the later pathology of the child, above all in what refers to autistic traits.

I want to make it clear at this point that any form of a child's ISO is much more difficult to discover than an adult's ISO. The child's ISO will change and develop over the years, according to the evolution of the child and his familial environment.

To our surprise, we have found the constant audition of classical music in the history of some of these children.

Our first approach to the family group is based on the hypothesis that, in the case of those children whose Ego-impacting sound we had not been able to find, we could look at the daily sound messages of the family group to the problem child. This might lead us to understand the existing messages and metamessages and to use some of them to open new communication channels.

It was evident that not all the components of the family group communicated in the same way, but that some were more successful than others. For example, sometimes the parents could not get any response from the problem child but one of the siblings or the nanny could (Fig. 21). This the parents themselves admitted.

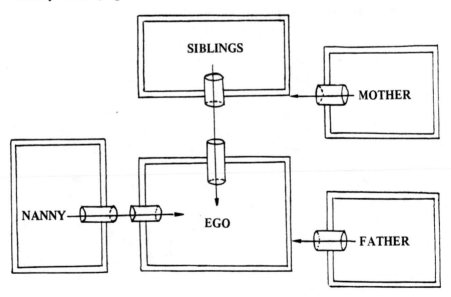

Figure 21.

The first technique we used was as follows: while we worked with the problem child as we have described in previous chapters, I summoned the parents, and during the first interview I commented on the type of therapy we were using with their child, telling them the results obtained up to that time in sufficiently simple terms to be understood by them.

Then I asked them for their collaboration and integration in our work. To do this I told them I would leave them alone in the same room in which the sessions were held, i.e. the blue room, with a recorder switched on but without the child, and I asked them to try to record all the forms of daily communication with their child (Fig. 22). I specified I was particularly interested in their being spontaneous, recording the normal way in which they addressed the child, including songs or games. I also told them that the recording would be heard by the child in the same way he heard other sounds. That is to say, I wanted to detect the communication cysts. Thus ended my first contact with the parents.

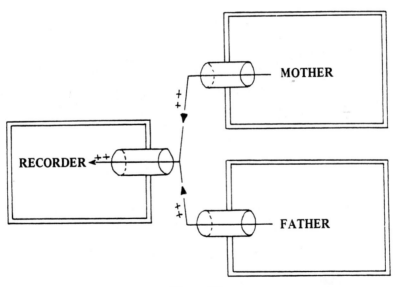

Figure 22.

The attitude of the parents and the recorded material were a real surprise. There were parents who told me, " ...I don't know what I'm going to record because we never speak to our child because he doesn't understand...he doesn't answer..." and another, "...I always say the same thing...."

In some recordings we found that parents emitted sounds or words every ten seconds; others spoke slowly, modulating the words and repeating everything several times "...waaaaateeeer... muuuuummy...daaaaaddy..." as if they were speaking to a deaf child.

Another parent, who could not say anything, reported the clinical and psychological history giving name and surname, born on such a day, normal birth, etc. Another parent, who knew beforehand from other parents what the session consisted of, brought a written paper on which he had put everything he was going to record. There were cases of parents who did not come to the appointment but who agreed to take the recorder home and make the recording there. There were still others, the fewest, where only one parent came, generally the mother.

Later I will describe fragments from the recording made by Mary's and Peter's parents and the children's response.

The second step was to work with the problem child, following the same procedure we had used with other sounds, i.e. playing with water and in the presence of the teacher (surrogate mother) and myself.

The response obtained was different in each case. We again detected a diagnostic differentiation between children with typically autistic traits and children with schizophrenic traits. The child with autistic traits did not give any responses, or these were reflected in a state of anxiety, anguish, or excitement.

On the other hand, the child with schizophrenic traits responded directly, e.g. if on the recording the mother began by saying "Hello, John, how are you?" the child answered "Well, Mummy." Another, on hearing his mother's voice said "That's Mummy." and answered some questions, laughed at some of the things the mother said, and did not play with the water during practically the whole session.

One of the problem children, on hearing the recording made at home together with his siblings, became markedly excited, left his place, touched different objects, moved from one place to another, switched the light on and off until he got into an armchair, and when he heard his father's voice, which insisted on his saying "Daddy," he said "caca"* and defecated.

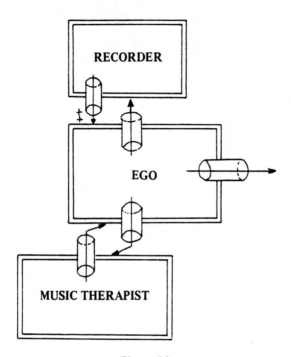

Figure 23.

In some children a clear difference could be seen between their reaction to their mother's and their father's voice. For example, one of the children, whose father brought in writing what he was going to record, on hearing his mother's voice became completely paralyzed, but when he heard his father's voice he returned to his stereotyped games and bizarre movements.

PETER'S CASE

I shall transcribe some fragments of the mother's and the father's recordings.

---

*Translator's note: "Caca" is used in Spanish both to tell the child to go to the bathroom and to mean "dirty" when telling the child not to touch something. As a result, children use it as an expletive when they want to be naughty and shock adults.

Mother's message:

"... Hello, Peter... What's the matter? Why are you crying? Come to mother... What's the matter... And Joseph? Where is he? Joseeeph... come Peter, sit down, get up, come don't lie on the floor... Peter, do you want to go to the bathroom, Do you want to pee? Run, run, run, run... (rhythmically) come, Peter, come, Peter. You must sleep, we're going to sleep. You must sleep, lie down, tomorrow you have to go to school... lie down here, by my side... Mummy is lying down with you (she begins to sing in a low melodious voice)... Mummy's Peter, Mummy's Peter, Daddy's Peter, Mummy's Peter, sweet Peter, good Peter, very good Peter, nana, nana, naana, naaana, nanana, nana, nana, na na na naa, look in the mirror, my beloved..." etc.

Father's message:

(In a strong, authoritarian voice) "... Hello, Peter. How are you? Come with Daddy, come, come, we're going to play. Be good, Peter, listen to Daddy, be good, eat your soup, be good, Peter. Oh, no, no not that, don't throw it, no, not that, no, pick it up, give it to me, no, no, don't throw it out, here, listen to Daddy, come, in the hand, no, no, pick it up again, no, no, don't throw it here, Very good, very good. Peter, sit down, sit down, there, don't move, be good, be careful, Daddy is getting angry, no, no, not that, I don't like that... give me your hand, give me your hand, we're going for a walk, be careful, Peter, let's go, careful of the staircase, slowly, Peter, very good, very good, Peter, Peter, put the light out, careful, good, very good, Peter..." etc.

Note how the whole recording is one long monologue of orders, threats, and classifications.

Peter's responses were the following:

On hearing the mother's message, and above all, when she began to sing the lullaby, he immediately assumed a fetal position, crouching near the teacher. When the mother said in an imperative tone "What are you doing, Peter. Get out of bed," he stood up immediately, went up to the recorder, and remained there, paralyzed.

During the father's message, he remained seated, serious, and began to play with his tongue, touching it, taking the whole of it in his hands, rubbing it; typical sterotyped attitude he adopts when he is anxious. He made some disconnected sounds.

As the responses were clearly defined, we repeated the examples, and Peter reacted in exactly the same way to each message. This enabled the music therapist to learn the mother's lullaby and was an excellent approach point, as, on hearing it, the child adopted the sleeping position similiar to the one he adopted on hearing his mother's message on the recorder, and then sat up waiting. He began to protest when the music therapist stopped singing, and this interplay made it possible to obtain a good connection with the music therapist, who was able to carry out very effective work with this child.

The step described allows us to speak of the second level of communication presented in this therapy.

Chapter 10

EFFECTS OF THE FIRST APPROACH TO THE FAMILY GROUP — CHANGES IN THE MESSAGE

A FTER A SHORT TIME WE BEGAN to note a change of attitude on the part of the parents, which consisted of asking us anxiously and enthusiastically what we could tell them about the results obtained with the recordings. It was the first time that these parents had been integrated actively with their children and had been interested in the results.

This led me to think that the technique described would be a very positive way of slowly including the parents in the therapeutic process of their child, without it being necessary, at the beginning, for them to see their child or the deep, verbalized conflicts of their own characteropathic personalities, which experience showed they flatly rejected. These parents frequently refused the suggestion to have individual, group, or even family therapy.

In view of these requests, I thought of the possibility of asking them to cooperate again in our therapy. So we again summoned each one of the pairs of parents. This happened about three or four months after their first collaboration.

During the second interview, we commented briefly on what they thought of their children, and then I told them about the results obtained with the recordings. I then made them listen to the recording they had made; that is, for the first time and three or four months later, they heard themselves (Fig. 24).

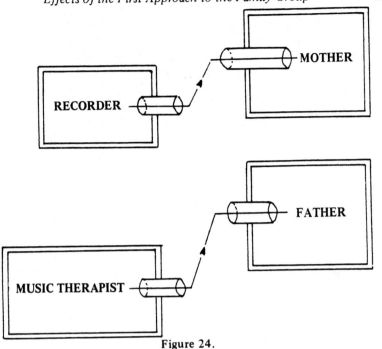

Figure 24.

Many parents found this retrospective auditory mirror test very positive because it quickly made them aware of the type of messages they were sending. Some exclaimed, for example, " ... How monotonous I am!" or "I recorded that?" We commented some aspects of the recording and of the responses of the children. Then, I asked them to make a new recording, but on the condition that it was to be different to the first one; that is, that they should modify the message, trying to think that the child would understand everything they were trying to tell him, or even that they should try and think and record all that they would like to tell their child and do not tell him because they believe that he will not understand or will not listen.

I again left them alone with the recorder switched on (Fig. 25).

The results of the recording of the parents' second message were dramatic and painful but of great prognostic value. It seemed that some of the parents had glimpsed those communication cysts. They were becoming aware of their existence, although they did not know yet which they were or what they were like.

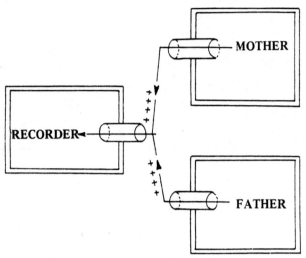

Figure 25.

As a result, many of the messages were completely changed. It could be noted that the problem child acquired another dimension within the family context, and stopped being what he was to become another type of child.

The characteristics of these new messages consisted of —

1. Sensation of deep affective mobilization.

2. Constant expressions of guilt, self reproaches, and apologies.

3. A new awareness of reality and disease.

One set of parents commented that they would be much more spontaneous in the second recording if they could do it in the common language they used at home. It was then that the child who spoke three languages was discovered: Armenian because it was the language of his parents, Turkish because it was the language of one of his grandparents, and Spanish so that he could adapt to the country.

They were allowed to record spontaneously in all three languages; the recording was much more fluid, of course, and from that time it was possible to change the therapeutical and pedagogic management of that child.

There were parents who did not change their message and others who exaggerated their characteropathies even more. In one case, the parents themselves began to look for forms of very bizarre communication, in general as if their child were deaf. Therefore, the first message was formed by modulated words that took several seconds to be pronounced, and in the second message they brought spontaneously speaking dolls to be recorded. All these forms readily became stereotyped.

On studying the strange material collected in the recordings, we were able to see the changes between the first monochord messages and the second in which we noted changes in sound intensity due to awareness of affective situations.

PETER'S CASE

I shall transcribe some fragments of Peter's parents' second message.

Father: "... Peterkin, today is Sunday and we're going for a walk... we're going with Eddie so that Peterkin you'd better get dressed... we're going to put on a pair of trousers... help me to put them on, come on, up go the trousers, there we are, so we can go for a walk. We're going to Ital Park... now give me your little hand, we're going walking... we're going in the lift. Peterkin, open the door, go in first. We're going to the car... Did you like the roundabout Peterkin? Good... You've been so good I'm going to buy you a balloon..."

The mother's second message does not show any important changes with respect to the first. In the father's, there is a change of voice, which has turned from authoritarian to affectionate and the verbal content which has become more intimate.

Peter's attitude to his father's second message was to remain seated at his place of work, seemingly very attentive. He made a move to touch his tongue only a very few times but did not do so. When he heard the mother's second message, his attitude was also very attentive and at the end when she said "bye," Peter clearly repeated "bye."

While this was going on, we started to observe notable changes in Peter. He integrated in his group quite well, ate all sorts of foods, responded to musical games and rounds, and to ball and ring games, and increasingly adapted to his daily activities.

These changes also occurred to the other children submitted to this treatment, and in my opinion this occurred not only because of the activities of the Institute but also because we were achieving a change of attitude in the parents.

Chapter 11

MUSIC THERAPY AND THE FAMILY GROUP: THE THERAPEUTIC COUPLE — LEVEL OF INTEGRATION

U P TO THIS POINT WE WORKED with the parents and the child separately, with ourselves acting as simple intermediaries at a distance. It became necessary to work with the parents and the problem child together, because if we obtained so many elements for the understanding of many phenomena that were occurring working separately, we could obtain much more working "in vivo."

My first concern, in order to start the family group on music therapy, was for the parents to accept it and to comply. I consequently suggested, as a trial, a brief work contract for only four meetings in all, leaving open the possibility of continuing these sessions or not, according to the results. So the parents were only required to come four times, for an hour and a half each time, during a period of from one to four weeks, i.e. we could meet four times in one week, or once a week, or twice, etc. It was up to the parents. This made it difficult for the parents to refuse, as they could arrange their timetable at work and other activities without creating too many problems and so gave less reasons for therapeutic resistance.

I had another interview with the parents in order to explain to them what we were doing. The terms I used, with some variations according to each case, were the following: "We are going to meet four times, here in the same place where we are talking now, together with your child and ourselves, i.e. the music therapist and myself. We will use some elements such as the instruments used by the music therapist and perhaps some balls or rings or something you may bring that you think may be useful. Our idea is to convert this into a sort of laboratory where we will be able to investigate what would be the best way or the best attitude or the best message to communicate with your child. So we will try to be spontaneous and to act freely, and at the end of each session we will comment on what has happened during the session."

This interview was held together with the music therapist. At the beginning of each session we talked about the expectations of the group and what fantasies they had about the future behavior of the problem child.

The session was held in the same room we had used for the previous sessions, after first removing any element that might hinder movement or the evolution of the session. So the only thing left was the big armchair and instruments, which we placed according to the requirements of each session (Fig. 26).

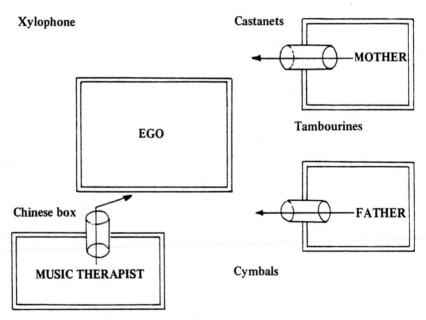

Figure 26.

The instruments used were the same as those used by the music therapist during his sessions, with the addition of the intermediary object that was used during the first stages. This was usually a simple percussion instrument such as clavés, the toc-toc, tambourines of different sizes, cymbals, recorder flute, bells, sistrums, etc., or Orff instruments.

There were sessions during which, because of the characteristics of the child, we either did not put anything or only one or two instruments because too many of them might scatter the child's and the parents' attention.

At the beginning of the session and before the child was brought in, we told the father to make himself comfortable, take off his jacket and so on; we asked the mother if she would like to put down her purse or any other disturbing element; i.e. we tried to make them feel at home. Once everyone was ready, the music therapist brought the child in.

At the beginning of the session I let the parents and the child act freely, maintaining an expectant and observing attitude. We allowed the spontaneous meeting of parents and child, which was, in general, free from any inhibition and showed us the genuine, typical manifestations of the parents towards the child. Reactions of anxiety or passiveness, which were generally the most characteristic, appeared clearly.

During the second stage of the session and depending on how the situation developed, we intervened in order to show the parents some form of approach, above all at moments of great frustration, or to stimulate the possibility of an effective integration. To achieve this objective it was sometimes enough to make a small imitative gesture, or some type of sound or movement, or some of the activities already carried out by the music therapist with the particular child to make it even easier for the child to come close or to respond.

At a third stage of the session we tried to play a game or make a round, stimulated by a song or rhythm, in which we all took part, i.e. the child, the parents, and the therapeutic couple formed by the music therapist and myself. This phase of the session was the most productive because of the immense pleasure it produced in the parents, who were able for the first time to be with their child half an hour or more, doing things together or playing.

When we finished the session, which depended on our perception of the way the child tolerated the situation, the music therapist took him back to the classroom and we remained some twenty minutes with the parents to comment on what had occurred and to make some observations on the manifest content of what had happened.

We did not make any interpretations at any time of unconscious mechanisms but limited ourselves to showing the stereotyped symptoms which could be clearly seen and which the parents were not conscious of, as they were too closely involved in the process. The response to this technique was highly beneficial and the results very productive.

For example, in a family group where both parents had clear and positive attitudes towards the child before the interview, it was observed that the father was incredibly passive to all the child's reactions and the mother, on the contrary, adopted an excited and demanding attitude, continually suggesting something new, changing and interrupting the games and proposing others.

After the first session and the comments made at the end, a change was observed, not only during the sessions but also — and this is more important — in the family milieu. The father understood that his attitude was peculiar to his character, and the mother acknowledged her anxiety. As a result, the tense atmosphere at home improved and they were able to communicate with the problem child, having understood many patterns of communication.

Another example is the couple who during the second recorded message brought talking dolls. This family group was really obsessed with being able to communicate with the problem child, and practically their only goal was that the child should say a few words. This obsession is characteristic of the parents of autistic children.

On starting the first session, we observed phenomena we had not been able to discover during the two years that the child had been coming to the Institute, either during the interviews or the monitoring, and which only appeared when we worked under the conditions described, i.e. parents and child in a nonverbal context.

We observed strange gestures made by the father when he spoke to his son, as if the latter were not only deaf but also partially blind. He opened his eyes wide and articulated slowly with his lips each syllable of the word he was saying. The faces he made were not only impressive but even frightening.

At the end of the session, we commented on what we had observed. The father asked if the child would really understand him if he spoke more quickly and without gestures. We elaborated this concern of the father's, and during the second session, a week later, he told us with surprise and pleasure that the child had in fact responded to the same order without any need of gestures or raising of voice.

In some cases, the father could not accept coming to the family group session, using work, lack of time, etc., as excuses. In other specially selected cases, I decided to work without the father, as I thought that all work on family integration must be very flexible. Integration must be obtained and not imposed, and this is a gradual process.

In our experience, the father would join the group after a time, tempted by the continuous messages that the mother took back about what was happening during the sessions of the family group. In spite of working only with the mother and the child during these sessions, the therapeutic couple formed by the music therapist and myself continued integrating them.

In one of these groups we observed that the mother was constantly kissing the child. These kisses and embraces paralyzed and inhibited any possibility of work. Faced with this attitude, she told us that she did this because she was afraid that her child would have a violent, aggressive, or convulsive episode at any moment or would start to cry desperately.

Little by little, as we had more sessions, the mother gave herself more freely to the rings, bodily games, and songs with us and the child until, during the last session of the first contract, she asked us to continue because she felt it was the first time that she could play with her child without any fear, as she felt an important container surrounding her. She left each session gratified and less anxious, which enabled her to accept her child's reactions spontaneously.

She insisted several times on showing us the difference that she felt with her marital therapy sessions, which left her feeling bitter and gave her a sensation of distaste. This mother improved her relations at home by making the father participate in what was happening to their son, thus indirectly integrating the father in the family group.

One of the positive aspects of the family group in music therapy was the possibility of giving it a defined container formed by the therapeutic couple, and the sound phenomena in which they could express themselves openly without fear of provoking immediate resistance. There were even cases in which work with the family group in music therapy enabled us to open the possibilities of the parents accepting a family group therapy that had been previously systematically rejected.

Before continuing with examples of family groups in music therapy, I think it would be useful to explain the origin of the therapeutic couple concept. By chance, due to the need of having the teacher (surrogate mother) work with me during the sessions in some cases, or the music therapist in others, we had formed in all the contexts in which we were working a real therapeutic couple, where we both carried out similar instructions but where we received from the patients different projections, which were clearly identifiable with the patient's projections towards his parents.

Frequently, for example, a child would reject me and look for protection in the music therapist and vice versa. This made it possible for the therapeutic container formed by the therapeutic couple to give greater spontaneity of expression to the problem children faced with our unexpected reactions. If the child expected an order from me or a repression and this did not occur, he changed the schema of the sterotyped message of the projected parent. The concept of the therapeutic couple is questioned by some authors because, it is argued, it produces jealousy and competition with the parents, above all when working with the child alone.

We have not noted this type of symptom in our experience; on the contrary, we rather felt that the parents were relieved at giving us the child. However, I have noted this jealousy in some family groups where the child preferred to establish contact with me or the music therapist, rejecting possibilities of doing so with the parents. This has been the exception; in general the parents tried to identify themselves with us as a therapeutic couple and went on to follow patterns that were very similar to ours.

In other cases, such as those where we worked with the mother alone, the therapeutic couple became a projection screen of the mother's infantile reactions, establishing good or bad contacts with us that were identifiable with her own parents.

PETER'S CASE

The parents accepted the family group sessions with pleasure. During the first session, the music therapist, who was ill, was replaced by the teacher (surrogate mother). This enabled us to establish the difference between a session carried out by a person not specialized in music therapy and the second session when the music therapist was present.

First Family Group Session

When the parents came in, I suggested they should make themselves comfortable, and I asked them if they wished to make any comments first or if they were ready for Peter. They said they were ready, so the teacher brought the child in.

As soon as Peter came in, both parents required him affectionately to give them a kiss, insisting several times on this until Peter complied. Once he had kissed them, they told him to clap his hands. When, after some insistence, he did so, the father turned to me and said, "... see, Doctor, see, he is clapping his hands... he is clapping his hands."

The sort of observation the father made is frequent during the first session of a family group, during which the parents try to show us some of their children's clear responses.

After insisting on other responses, the teacher also began to show Peter's skills to the parents. She made him play ball, sing, move, etc. Peter reacted sporadically with screams or by clinging with his perspiring hands to those of the teacher, looking for protection.

After twenty minutes, Peter went back to his classroom and we commented the vicissitudes of the session with the parents. I tried to make them see everybody's anxiety to make Peter respond as an outstanding fact, each of them trying to show their own skill in dealing with Peter, without respecting Peter's own particular time, which required special patience for each response. I showed them how he was required to kiss, clap his hands, play, etc., in a few short minutes.

The teacher also recognized her identification with the parents by trying to show off Peter's skills.

This recognition of the special time of each child with his parents is one of the transcendental observations in this type of child. In other words, it is like leading the parents to discover slowly and for themselves what their child's ISO is.

During the second session, the parents brought some toys that Peter usually played with at home. During this session, the music therapist who worked with Peter during individual music therapy sessions was present.

Peter came in, brought by the hand by the music therapist. The parents adopted a more passive attitude. Peter was undecided and afraid. He observed everything and groaned from time to time.

When the father told him to kiss his mother, Peter emitted more intense sounds and still seemed undecided. We waited in silence for a little while longer, and Peter came up to the music therapist and tried to take her hands. She took advantage of this moment to sing very gently: "Hello, Peter?" (Fig. 27).

Figure 27.

This was the song that made it possible to connect during the music therapy sessions. Peter liked this type of song very much.

Then the music therapist sang "Caminando" (Walking) (Fig. 28) rhythmically.

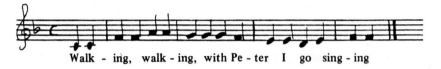

Walk - ing, walk - ing, with Pe - ter I go sing - ing

Figure 28.

Peter automatically began to walk, and on my indication the parents joined him and walked behind him. In this way the four of us walked in Indian file behind Peter.

When the music therapist stopped singing, Peter stopped walking, and when she started singing again, he immediately started walking, followed by his parents. The music therapist took the tambourine and a drumstick and beat the rhythm of the song. Peter came up to the music therapist, took the drumstick, and began to beat with precision the tambourine held by the music therapist.

But he beat a very clear, new rhythm, which made the parents imitate him. I brought up two more tambourines, and Peter beat first on one then on the other, complicating the rhythms but always following the humming of the music therapist.

Then came a moment of great excitement, when the parents were very surprised by their son's skill and concentrated on the same rhythm Peter was beating. The latter was also beating a tambourine held by his father.

I want to clarify again that Peter seemed to have simultaneously autistic symptoms, brain damage, and great difficulties in motor balance in the legs and hands, but that these disappeared when he entered this sort of rhythmic extasis.

The rhythm began fading until it disappeared. We tried to form a ring with the parents, but Peter immediately freed himself and started beating the tambourines again. This session lasted 40 minutes.

The comments relating to the parents' discovery that Peter had a motor skill showed they were really surprised. They went away, very pleased and with the sensation that Peter was not a little animal without sphincter control.

The difference between the first session in which the teacher took part and the second with the music therapist was evident. The richness of the sound element opened the child and the parents and decreased the anxiety produced during the first session, during which verbalization prevailed.

The third session was similar to the previous ones. During the last session the parents arrived punctually. They were pleased with the results obtained, and they noted changes in their son such as his managing to run better and muttering imitative words more clearly. Moreover, the mother managed to control her anxiety to feed him so that the child began to eat solids by himself.

The last point is another positive aspect of these family groups where we continue acting in the family by means of simple formulations of clear and defined manifestations which occurred during the session.   .

When Peter came, the parents, much calmer now (they had learned to wait), observed. Peter looked at the instruments, rubbed his ears and his tongue, and sat down near the tambourine. He took up the drumstick and tried to make a beat.

The music therapist began to intone "Hello, Peter." Peter managed to babble with a guttural intonation; the parents came up to him at this moment and accompanied him. There was no need to encourage them. Peter always used the right hand, giving the impression that he had difficulty in coordinating his left hand. That is why we tried to make him work in a vertical position, as this way it was easier to use the left hand.

I made a sign to the music therapist to join Peter and we all tried to work in a vertical position.

The music therapist intoned "Walking, walking," and the parents and I began to walk around Peter. (This game is played at group music therapy sessions.) After three turns, Peter got up spontaneously and followed the file in a disorderly fashion. In this position, we again tried to beat the rhythm, each of us taking a tambourine, and Peter began to beat very characteristic rhythms with his drumstick, using the three tambourines. This gave special color to the rhythm which was generated only by Peter, to the surprise of his parents.

The music therapist imitated the rhythm with the flute and tried to vary it. Peter responded to the variations but immediately returned to his own rhythm. It clearly responded to his rhythmic ISO.

The music therapist left the flute and began to clap the rhythm. Peter responded much better to the clapping, became excited, left the drumsticks, and went to the music therapist to take her hands, not to stop her but to get the drive to clap too. To the parents' surprise, Peter clapped the music therapist's rhythm with both hands, synchronizing perfectly.

We all began to clap the rhythm with increasing intensity; Peter walked between us, sometimes stopped, and then went on and was very excited. From time to time, he emitted guttural rhythms; the music therapist imitated these guttural sounds and the parents began to imitate them too; we were all in Peter's ISO. An intense atmosphere of communication was produced in which a perfectly compact group could be perceived.

The session ended, and Peter returned to his usual place.

The parents regained their lost faith, and they felt acutely the need to go on working with Peter. I suggested that within one or two months we should return and carry out a similar experience. Both parents accepted with pleasure. We got the father, an industrialist who was very busy, to feel the need of continuing the experience for himself and not to interpose any obstacles of time.

This is one of many examples of our family group sessions with music therapy. I think it is an ideal technique to begin the integration of the family nucleus in the therapeutic action and a way of opening communication channels between the problem child and the parents by breaking communications cysts.

Appendix

MUSIC THERAPEUTICAL TREATMENT OF
A BLIND CHILD WITH
SERIOUS BEHAVIOR DISORDERS

MARÍA ROSA ALFONSÍN de SURMANI

M.'S CASE HISTORY

In this paper I shall report the case of a blind patient with serious personality disorders.

Patient: M.
Sex: Male
Age: 7
Family group: Mother, father, sister of 6, twins of 4, and a maternal grandmother.

M. was born blind due to a malformation (anhyrridia), which was later complicated by glaucoma. During his first year of life he had to be operated on four times on each eye; he was first operated on when he was a month and half old.

Operations: 1. Glaucoma, both eyes; 2. Opening of the lens, both eyes; 3. Repetition of prior operation; 4. Vitreous humor graft in one eye.

From the age of three and a half, M. went to a school for the blind, joining the preschool group. His attendance was irregular until he was five years old. According to his teacher, M. was a

Maria Rosa Alfonsin de Surmani is a music therapist from the School of Paramedical Disciplines of the Medical School of The Salvador University, Buenos Aires, Argentina.

problem child, but he managed to communicate with her and the group within his capabilities. This communication disappeared around seven years of age.

He entered into crisis easily, crying and screaming disconsolately. Before any request, however simple, M. said, "Finished," or "I don't feel like it." When any of his schoolmates came up to him to play, he said, "good-bye."

Due to serious personality disorders and the impossibility of adapting to the institutional environment, M. could not continue his studies. As M. liked music (he spent a long time at home sitting in an armchair, listening to records) and because of his serious communication problems, music therapy was suggested as a first therapeutic possibility and approach to the learning process.

He was sent to me by his doctor in May, 1972, when he was seven.

Music Therapy Questionnaire

At the age six, M. had started psychotherapeutic treatment, three sessions a week. During the first interview with the mother and in later interviews with the grandmother I drew up his music therapy questionnaire.

The following are the mother's textual answers:

1. *What nationality is the father?* Italian.

2. *And you?* Spanish.

3. *What is your and your husband's favorite music?* His father likes classical music and opera. I quite like opera. I prefer classical music, particularly symphonies, folklore, modern music, and tangoes.

4. *What sound experiences did you have during your pregnancy?* None.

5. *And during birth?* None.

6. *What were M.'s first days like?* He was quiet. According to his grandmother, he never cried like a normal child; his crying was rather like a complaint. He brought up all his food. The grandmother said that after consultations and the diagnosis of blindness, the mother suffered a severe breakdown.

7. *What lullabies did you sing to him?* I sang to him but never to put him to sleep. I liked singing.

8. *Did you rock him while you were singing?* M. loved being moved. Now he is in constant movement.

9. *What type of music did he listen to?* He preferred popular songs and children's songs to classical music.

10. *What type of music did he reject, or what type gave him pleasure?* Since he was small he rejected any wind instrument; he became hysterical; now he accepts them better. He rejects the noise of the vacuum sweeper, polishing machine, and the saw at the butcher's.

11. *And you, the parents, how did you react to sounds and noises?* No way in particular.

12. *What does he remember from the first three years of his life?* Popular songs and fashionable music. Now he asks for Mamie Blue and Soleil. He knows how to sing in English, Spanish, and Italian.

13. *What typical sounds does he hear at home (slamming of doors, screams, chewing noises, tics that make a sound, murmurs, etc.)?* Normal.

14. *What did he hear during the night?* At home we can hear the train and motor launches, but they don't bother him. He loves going in a launch.

15. *Does he have any bodily sounds?* He makes sounds with his body. He doesn't make any sound with his mouth. In general, he is content; when he is quiet, he becomes anxious and ends up by crying.

16. *What type of musical education do you have?* We haven't studied music but we love it. His father sings out of tune but, he likes it very much.

17. *Did M. have any music lessons?* No, he didn't.

18. *What were his contacts with musical instruments like?* He panicked when he first heard the accordion but not afterwards. He was given a very beautiful one, sent from Italy, and rejected it. When he was two he could accompany a samba with a guitar very well, then he stopped playing himself but he wanted me to play it.

19. *What is his attitude to music now?* He likes to listen to music, seated in an armchair for a long while. He always listens to tapes recorded with different sounds and noises. He listens to them very attentively and recognizes them all.

20. *Does he associate anything with sounds or fragments of music?* No.

21. *What type of music does he prefer?* He likes the sound of the guitar very much. Although he rejects the harmonica, he likes to listen to it when his sister plays it and moves to the beat of the music.

22. *Does he show preference for any instruments?* No.

Testing of the Nonverbal Context

The idea of the first interview with the patient was to observe his instrumental possibilities to find an intermediary object and his time characteristics, i.e. to discover his ISO.

The instruments placed on the table were the following: sistrums, triangles, bells, chin chin, recorder flute, tambourine, clavés, and Chinese box. The open piano was standing near the table.

M. came in with his mother.

I said, "Hello, M. how are you? Do you know my name?" M. answered me through clenched teeth: "Maria Rosa."

In the mean time, the mother was taking off his pullover and was telling him she would be coming back to fetch him in a short while. M. repeated, "You're coming to fetch me?"

We took the mother to the door and returned to our place of work. I knew M. needed an armchair as a frame of reference to be able to carry out any kind of activity. I therefore told him he had several armchairs, big and small, and that we would try them all. He clung to my hands and I took him to the armchairs. M. repeated, "to the armchair... to the armchair."

Then I gave him the first instructions for the testing. I told him that on the table there were various musical instruments, that he could do what he liked with them, and that later we would listen to music.

M. repeated everything I said and added some phrases of his own, such as, "the center... we're in the center... elevator." He did this because they lived in the country and he liked coming to town and going up in the elevator.

I brought him near to the instruments and M. said, "...afterwards to the armchair." All he said was said with decision, a characteristic of his.

It is important to explain that sighted children who are being tested should not be taken to the table with the instruments. A simple gesture is enough. The blind, however, must be led to the table.

When he started touching the instruments, he became excited and seemed pleased. He already knew the clavés, the tambourine, and the bells. I went with him around the table, helping him to find and pick up the other instruments. His attitude consisted of touching an instrument briefly, leaving it, and saying, "...finished..." and then running to look for other instruments and doing exactly the same.

He went around the table again, repeating the same procedure; then he said, "to the armchair." It was then that I led him up to the piano. He felt it all over, moving his body to a given rhythm. I took advantage of this and began to play a song for children entitled "Little horse."

M. accompanied me, beating the keys with his fingers, and immediately said, "close it." He took the lid of the piano and closed it. As he insisted on going back to the armchair, I accompanied him and left him to put on a record. While I was doing this, he was bouncing on the armchair.

While he was listening to a Chopin waltz, he continued bouncing in a stereotyped way. I tried to take his hands and to make some movements with him, but he rejected this. He continued bouncing without taking any interest in me.

I put on a second musical fragment, but his attitude did not change. We finished with the musical pieces, and I waited for a while in silence but, as I saw that M. did not stop bouncing on the armchair, I went up to the piano and improvised a simple score, following the rhythm of his bouncing. His immediate response was to scream louder and louder, all the time interrupting himself to say "don't shout... it is nasty to shout..." On seeing M.'s state of anguish, I went up to him affectionately. M. took my hands and pinched them so hard they bled. Suddenly he grabbed my neck and hurt me.

In view of this and being unable to calm him any other way, I went to the gramophone and put on Liszt's Love Song. When M. heard the music, he stopped screaming and began rocking his body sideways from right to left. When the record stopped, M. said "finished?" and started rocking himself again. At this moment, a bell rang. The thirty minutes of the session were up, and his mother had come to fetch him. I explained to him that it was his mother who had come to fetch him and that we would go and open door together.

M. started screaming heartrendingly; it was then that I asked him if he wanted to stay while I went to the door. He did not say anything but went on screaming, clinging to me and scratching my hands without letting me move. While he was screaming, he was saying "don't shout..." Finally, I told him energetically that if he did not want to come with me, he should wait there until I opened the door to his mother.

When his mother came in, M. followed me, screaming. He calmed down little by little, and when he left he was able to say goodbye quietly.

Evaluation

During my contact with the patient I was able to observe –

Echolalia. Obsessive tendency to remain in the armchair while he was listening to music.

Recognition of nearly all the instruments, which he almost immediately abandoned. The use of the third person when speaking about himself.

Rejection of the piano and particularly of wind instruments.

Great discharges of uncontrolled movements of the limbs.

Stereotyped movements with his hands and fingers.

During the review of the questionnaire and the music therapy test which I made with the physician-psychiatrist, the following objectives and instructions to be followed during treatment emerged.

Objectives

To achieve communication with the patient through sounds and music which would make it possible to break the blockade and the pathological communication channels that kept the patient isolated from the surrounding world.

To carefully avoid creating cysts within those channels with the same sound and music elements.

To establish a new relationship, which would enable M. to develop new patterns of behavior, modifying the pathological symbiosis with the mother, which we later also observed with the maternal grandmother.

To channel his sterotyped movements to achieve intentional patterns of movement.

Instructions

To avoid identification with the patient's anxiety.

To try to give very simple and short instructions.

To take advantage of the percussion instruments as intermediary objects.

Not to use the piano to begin with.

To respond to the patient's screams with the echo of some instrument.

To make movements accompanying the songs.

To try to establish a purely nonverbal context.

Finally, a music therapy treatment was programmed for two individual sessions a week.

EVOLUTION DURING THE FIRST YEAR OF TREATMENT – EXAMPLE OF A MUSIC THERAPY SESSION

During almost two months M. remained seated in the same armchair, listening to records. In view of this rejection of instruments, I tried to record different rhythms on the tambourine. When M. heard the recording, he exclaimed with surprise, "the instruments on a record?" Thus, little by little, his passive attitude became more active. Whatever he did, beating an instrument for example, he immediately stopped, saying "finished!"

In general, he rejected any attempt of mine to communicate, saying "I don't want to" in his own particular tone (Fig. 29).

I   don't want to

Figure 29.

He often had fits of crying and screaming, during which he told himself "one shouldn't scream. It's naughty to scream," while he continued screaming. Feeling that M. was afraid, I used to go up to him. When I did so, he attacked me, scratching and pinching me until my hands bled.

I shall now transcribe the session during which the first changes occurred. During that session, I decided to try to eliminate the recorded musical phenomena, because I considered that the patient was using them as a defense against communication and that they produced communication cysts.

Synthesis of the Session

M. came in and asked me to take him to the armchair and to put on records. He remained seated, listening to Chopin's Nocturne in E flat. I accompanied him by beating the rhythm on some instrument and inviting him to do the same. I was immediately rejected. In spite of this, I continued.

When I tried to give him an instrument, he screamed and threw away everything that I gave him. In the meantime, he said "the cap? the cap of the train? the cap of the *ravioles?*" I did not understand what he wanted, so I said I did not have the cap.

M. insisted. Then I reached for the plates of the sistrum and told him that these were the caps I had and that they made a noise. M. said, "Caps that make a noise?" I took advantage of this to sound the instrument. M. screamed and threw the sistrum at me. He again asked for the caps, and I explained he had thrown them on the floor.

In the meantime, the music continued, Chopin Waltz in C major.

To whatever I suggested, M. answered "I don't want to." When the music stopped, M. said "More." I took advantage of this to start singing, "M. is a child who comes to play. M. is a child who comes to sing, sing, sing, lalala..." (Fig 30). M. said "More." I started singing again, trying to get him to imitate me. M. began speaking aloud and ended with a yell: "more? more? more?" I answered with my own "more? more? more? (Fig. 31).

As I continued singing, his voice became plaintive and he said, "more, more, more record, more music." I tried changing the song, singing a tune he liked. He did not listen to me and turned his back, screaming heartbreakingly. I explained that the record was finished. M. said, "more record! The record is finished!" I offered him the tambourine and he said, "I don't want to." The same occured with the Chinese box, the small cymbals, etc. He always repeated "I don't want to" in the same tone of voice. I took up the tambourine and began to play. I invited him to beat on it, and he began to shout "I don't want to"; I answered "But I do want to," and I continued playing.

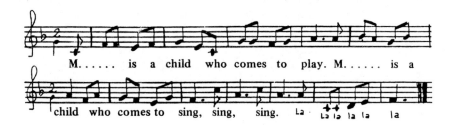

M. . . . . . is a child who comes to play. M. . . . . . is a child who comes to sing, sing, sing. La . La la la la la

Figure 30.

more, more, more

Figure 31.

M. said, "We're going to throw it on the floor?" I went on beating, and he continued shouting and insisted "We're going to throw it on the floor?" I went on beating, and he repeated "We're going to throw it on the floor?" I answered "I don't want to" in the same tone (Fig. 32).

We'll throw it on the floor. I don't want to.

Figure 32.

Suddenly he seemed to be expecting something, and little by little he calmed down and spoke to me more quietly, always maintaining the same modulation of voice. I took advantage of this and made changes of intensity, modulation, and accentuation in the same phrase.

During fifteen minutes we played the game of question and answer. During this time, M. stopped his heartbreaking screaming and spoke in his normal tone of voice; at times, he even imitated my singing in a low voice, interspersing pauses of up to a minute in an expectant attitude, during which it was possible to observe a total integration in my communication channel.

At a given moment I changed the game, saying, "We won't throw it on the floor?" (to see if M. would repeat what I said).

He was silent for a while and then went back to his "We're going to throw it on the floor?" We went on for a time with question and answer, and then I began to sing "We're going to throw it on the floor, I don't want to" (Fig. 33).

We'll throw it on the floor. I don't want to

Figure 33.

He listened to me very attentively. After a short silence, he interrupted my song, saying "We're going to throw it on the floor" (affirmative). This was the end of the session.

Commentary

I achieved my objective during this session: to establish direct contact with M. and to eliminate the musical element that kept him isolated. This contact was established when I managed to introduce myself into the melodic and tonal context of his expressions. In this way, his anxiety and screaming diminished and turned into a game of questions and answers.

After this session:

a. He began to be interested in songs and instruments, accompanying me briefly on the piano or some other instrument.

b. He refused to use the flute or the harmonica. The first contacts with these instruments were aggressive, i.e. when he blew, he
bit the mouthpiece, made faces, and then cleaned his mouth. I
then began to do breathing exercises, first sitting back in an armchair, then, insofar as M. allowed it, on the carpet. He breathed
compulsively. Gradually, following my example, he relaxed, until
his breathing was almost normal. Later, I again insisted on the
flute, while I asked M. to blow the rhythm of a simple tune he
knew well, I blocked the corresponding sounds with my fingers.
In this way he gradually lost fear of wind instruments.

I also used the harmonica because he found it easier to produce sounds, playing at emitting low and high notes, and could
hold it himself.

As he did not use his hands, and when he touched objects he
did so from above as if he were afraid of hurting himself, I insisted
that he should pick up the instruments by himself, thus working
on his fine motor functions.

We thought, along with the physician who treated him, that
learning the wind instrument technique would make it easier for
him to learn Braille later on.

c. I observed that on walking he dragged his feet and always
put the same foot forward as if he were rocking himself. This produced a double-time progress because he went one step forward,
then half a step back.

I pointed this out to him and asked him to make another
sound on walking — to raise first one foot then the other, marking
each step as he moved forward, while I accompanied him with a
song, "walking, walking, with M. I go singing" (Fig. 34).

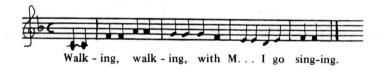

Walk - ing,   walk - ing,   with M . . . I go sing-ing.

Figure 34.

In this way he started walking, feeling more sure of himself,
replacing the forward and backward movement by walking for-

ward with both feet. Later he was able to learn how to jump with both feet together and to jog.

d. One of M.'s behavioral patterns was to refuse any new suggestion because he felt unable to carry it out. One way of expressing this anxiety was a long scream followed by crying. After various attempts, he changed his behavior, and the new achievement made him happy. In this way he assimilated new elements such as the ring, the stick, and the rope, which he then included in his games.

At the same time, M. was included in Dr. Benenzon's therapy. M. was very excited by sound stimuli, which either exacerbated or inhibited his hand and arm hyperkinesia according to what he heard and stopped all movement at the beginning of a new sound or tune.

He used to say a few words and happily played with water. In other words, he did not behave like an autistic child but like one with schizoid traits.

I shall now transcribe the first messages of M.'s mother and father.

When Dr. Benenzon gave them the instructions, they remained alone in the blue room and recorded.

Mother:

"M. Do you want me to sing Ramon's song? well... Ramon, heart of mine, Ramon, heart of mine, heart of mine Ramon. Chip pon. If you had married, If you had married when I told you, Chip pon. You would not be now, you would not be now sitting on your balcony, Chip pon. Four carts went by, four carts went by loaded with munitions, Chip pon. Two for Saragossa, two for Saragossa and two for Ramon, Chip pon. Did you like it, M? Darling, you want to go boating but we can't go boating every Sunday, it's not possible every day... come, come with Mother to the kitchen; we'll make some *escalopes*... Ugh! look at you..., oh! it doesn't matter if you're dirty, you can wash later... See how nice it is to cook?... what d'you want to play?... At being a baby, Ugh! always at being a baby, ... you must play at some thing else... it's boring always playing at being a baby... M. it's time to eat, come on, hurry up... oh! Mummy has the prettiest thing... what a lovely boy... Whose child is this lovely boy?... come on, M. go and play with your brothers and sisters at being sailors... good... very good, M.... Now I'm going tell you a story... Once upon a time there was a cat which had a head of cloth and a tail upside down. D'you want me to tell you the story again?... Now, you tell me a story... let's see, come on, M. be a good boy...come on, tell me a story...go to the bathroom, bathroom, you mustn't wait until the last minute to go to the bathroom; then it's too late...see what happens, you have to run, run to go to the bathroom... No, M., you can't speak like that, you must say the whole word like... if not, you can't be understood, one can't understand anything if you mumble..."

Father:

"Hello, M.... I bet you don't know who I am?... let's see if you reconize me... come I'll squeeze you with all my strength... you're strong. Give me your arm... Let's see... put your arm here, come... Did I squeeze you hard?... it hurts, you say help, help and I let you go... come on, one, two, three... The other day when we went for a walk and had an ice cream, on Sunday, remember? You got in the car and you went to the back and you started to scream. Ugh, ugh, how did you do it? And your brothers and sisters pulled your leg... I had to stop, you had to get out to come in front and then we went to have an ice cream. I bet you don't remember what ice cream you had?... Well, if you remember, you'll tell me later.., afterwards, we went, went, went... for a long drive and you were jumping and kicking, you kicked the whole car, the new car and I got angry. I shouted at you and then you quieted down. You know I don't like it when you break my car, you must be careful because it is very expensive... There's no school on Friday this weekend because it's a holiday, then we'll go for a long, long drive into the country... Good!... How happy you are, you're going to meet the lady, remember?, who you call aunt and she's going to get angry and she'll speak Italian to you... well, after that you'll go out and see your Granny... What are you going to do with Granny? You'll go for a walk, you'll go and see the hens, ride the pony, let's see if you remember what you're going to do? You won't want to come back... look, we'll only be a few days and then... we'll be there Friday, Saturday and Sunday. On Monday you have to go to school. M., let's play at being a doctor... let's see, come, lie down here... open your mouth and show me... your throat, say aaaaa... good, now turn round and I'll give you an injection, one, two, and ready... Did it hurt? Now we'll take your temperature to see if you have a high temperature, give me your arm. Have you put the thermometer under your arm? Now we're going to count up to ten, you count up to ten, let's see if you remember, I take it out..."

That was the end of M.'s parents' first recording.

When M. heard his mother's message, he immediately responded, "That's Mummy!" and he answered all the questions that the mother asked; he laughed at certain insinuations and did not play with the water. When he heard his father's voice, he was more serious. It was some time before he said "that's Daddy," and then he played with the water.

After some months had passed, Dr. Benenzon again summoned the parents and, after making them listen to the recording. he asked them to try to change the previous message, suggesting they should say everything they wanted to tell M. that they had never told him before.

I shall transcribe the mother's message. What she said in a completely different tone of voice was the following:

Mother's second message:

"... Hello, darling... you know that Rolando [that is Dr. Benenzon's name] said I had to come here today at three to make a recording and suddenly I was afraid... I thought I would not be able to think of anything to say to you, ... because, you know, mummies are also afraid... not only children... me too. I realized, when I listened to the previous recording that we spoke very little... that I only gave orders or asked questions... but that we spoke very little... and I want to tell you things so often but I think you won't understand them, that you won't understand them and... and today Rolando made me understand that there are many ways of making you understand things and of explaining... for example, a few days ago, when we were driving, either coming or going to school, I saw that the trees were so green, that the tender leaves were beginning to come out, the sky was so clean and the sun so shining and I would have liked to tell you all these things and for you to see them and... and feel... but I didn't know how to tell you... don't think this only happens to me when I'm with you, it happens when I'm with your brothers and sisters too, I don't know if the rhythm of the life we lead, the hurry, the shopping, the comings and goings, the days go by and we speak so little... but you know, it's not easy, at least not for me it's not easy, it's very difficult, I realize we're living very badly, and I imagine what I want most is to help you as much as I can, but I realize I need others to help me, that I can't alone, but I'm trying, I'm doing something to get that calm, that assurance I'm lacking, and to transmit it to your brothers and sisters... I'm a little sentimental today, perhaps because of the day, which is like this, so cloudy, warm, damp, heavy, I love you all very much and really I want to do my best for you, I realize I don't know how, that there are many things I don't know, but I want to learn them, you know, there is something I want to tell you and I didn't, which made me very happy; after Wednesday I'm going to come every afternoon to school and we are going to work together with Nestor, the three of us, so Mummy will learn together with you, don't you think it will be nice ... I was thinking that possibly my mistake, not speaking to you and your brothers and sisters too, is that I think you will not understand me, that you will not understand my questions, for example, and I would love it if you'd tell me more about what you do at school, what you do with your little friends, then I too would ask you about them, how you are, if you are happy... because, truly, above all things I want you to be happy. You will help me."

This is how the recording ends. It was the first time that the mother spoke to M. as if he were an older child, dropping the childish prattle she normally used to communicate with him.

On hearing the recording, M. gave the impression of a child who had been impressed or paralyzed as, in spite of his hyperkinesia, he remained motionless during the whole of the recording, did not play with the water, and only listened.

As from that moment, some changes were observed in the mother's relations with M., which in turn caused behavioral and management changes in M., which were not always pleasant for those who were around him, since he sometimes became very aggressive; however, he became very positive in his manifestations.

LATER EVOLUTION AND INTEGRATION IN A GROUP – THE FAMILY GROUP

As M. began to feel more assured, he began to –

a. Find out about the place of work; he opened doors and tried to know all the space that surrounded him both in and out of the office.

b. Whenever he found something new, M. asked, "This is...?" and waited for me to finish the sentence. This game was played in his communication with his mother. *Example:* M.: "We're going now?" Mother's answer: "To the drugstore." M. tried to play this game with everything he wanted to relate with. The mother was asked to reform this type of communication, which would lead M. to say the whole sentence. This has not been fully solved, as the mother insists on the previous type of relationship.

c. The same occurred with the use of the third person. At home, he was spoken to like this: Mother: Mummy is going to take you to the park (instead of saying "I'm going to take you to the park"). Grandmother: "Granny is going to give you a bath" (instead of saying "I'm going to give you a bath"). Gradually this disappeared and M. managed to distinguish between mine and yours. M. is used in interfamilial relations as the container of the problems existing in the family (mother, father, grandmother relations). This is aggravated by the father's rejection of M., which implies a lack of identification with the father image. This image is displaced towards the grandmother, who exercises the paternity rights.

d. Conversation through singing was changed; when M. had to answer either affirmatively or negatively, he did so in the form of a question: "Yes?" "No?" (in spite of the fact he knew the correct way to answer). Insecurity led him to get the other person to affirm or deny in his stead. This attempt not to assume responsibility for his answers changed little by little. When he said "Yes?" I repeated the questions, and M. would answer "Yeees," as if doubting what he was affirming, but with more assurance.

e. His voice was very childish, sounding like a falsetto (this was encouraged by his mother who, in her relationship with M., tried to make him stay a baby).

f. Incomprehensible soliloquies, laughter, and murmurs were often heard.

g. On being asked what he wanted to do, he would repeatedly say "something"; on being asked what that something was, he answered "something; I don't know what." Later, he was able to decide without difficulty what he wanted to do.

h. He also changed his use of deferred echolalia.

At the age of eight, M. entered the Instituto de Nivelación Pedagógica, where he was introduced to approach techniques to daily tasks.

I was able to observe how M. handled himself when faced with a group as I was working as a music therapist at that Institute. M. continued private treatment with me at the same time.

Adaptation to a group was not easy, as M. said "good-bye?" whenever a child came up to him. He was aggressive and often screamed.

It is important to remember he was the only blind child in a group of children with personality disorders.

As he rejected physical contact, I used a wooden hoop and a rope as a linking object. Motivated by the songs, M. made, together with another child, such movements as hammock, cart, train, etc. In the same way, he played a rhythmic or melodic echo on percussion instruments. He accepted singing in a group or alone but only for a short time.

He only communicated briefly with the group. M. was very frightened of any change. He would say "No, you don't want to, no?" He refused to be moved from his work table and if he was left without anything to do, he would cross his arms and lay his head on them. In spite of this, we gradually managed to make positive changes in his behavior.

When we assessed M.'s behavior at the end of a year with Dr. Benenzon, we agreed to have four family group sessions.

First Family Group Session

I went to look for M. to take him to the blue room where Dr. Benenzon and his parents were waiting for him. On the way, I explained that Mummy, Daddy, and Rolando were there together to play for a while with him and there were also some musical instruments.

On going in, he went up to each one to say hello; then I led him to the table where the instruments were. He touched many of them but did not seem decided about any of them. The mother immediately touched the Chinese box and said she had not seen one before. In the meantime M. picked up the flute, caressed it, but did not put it to his mouth.

The father was undecided, and it was then that the physician indicated with a gesture he should pick one up. As he had played the flute as a child, he chose that instrument and emitted some sounds. Smilingly, the mother accompanied him.

M. did not do anything but kept the flute. After a while he put down the flute and picked up the triangle and accompanied his parents from time to time. Every time the mother asked him to play, M. dropped the instrument. In the end, M. said in his usual tone of voice and threateningly, "See, if you wet yourself! ... ," repeating the phrases he usually heard his mother say.

The mother answered, "Let's not speak about that now..."

The parents tried to play other rhythms, but M. did not accompany them. The mother became anxious. She repeated, "Louder, it can't be heard..." (she referred to the instrument M. was holding) "Do you always work like this with Maria Rosa?..."

After a while, the mother asked M. to sing a song together but M. resisted her, remaining completely mute. I then asked M. to play with the hoops. I gave a hoop to each one and suggested we play the game of house. This game consists in placing a hoop on the floor, and each one of the players stands in it. Then he walks outside the house (the hoop) and returns to his own or goes to visit one of the others. This game is appropriate for M. because it enables him to increase his tactile perception at the foot level. It goes with a song. So, while I sang, they all went for a walk outside the hoops, and when the song ended they all returned to their own hoops.

The father's attitude to this game was not to accept the rules and to remain passive. On the other hand, the mother tried to help M. constantly, showing him where he had to go or what he had to do. M. managed well and was happy.

I suggested the game of hammock, which M. knew well. It consists of sitting on the ground, touching the soles of the feet of the other person and holding hands and rocking forward and back.

He did it first with me then he tried to do it with his mother. When playing with her he tended to lie down on the floor and remain in that position.

We also tried holding the hoops. The father did not want to do it. Finally, we played the little train, in which the whole family group took part. When M. was placed behind his mother, he acted naturally, but when he was behind his father, he hang on to his jacket and let himself be drawn.

To say goodbye, I started to sing "The Last Tram," a song we use in group work to say goodbye. However, when I took him by the hand to go out, he refused. He clung to his mother. The father asked him to kiss him and to hug him. M. refused. In the end, we left singing.

We made the comments with the parents, first the father's sensation of being observed and controlled, which prevented him from being more at ease, and then the mother's attitude of not allowing M. to develop his own initiative, trying to help him or telling him what he had to do or not to do. The mother accepted this commentary with the typical reaction she showed at home when dealing with M.

Family Group Second Session

When we came into the blue room, I took M. up to the instruments. The mother picked up the tambourine but immediately put it back and said it was better to let M. choose first. She was told to act spontaneously, not controlling what she thought she should not do.

Finally, each member of the group took up an instrument, and then I asked them to sit on the floor. As he was sitting down, M. said, "the armchair is better..." The father sat on a chair. I began to sing songs that M. knew. They all sang, except M. who accompanied us with the claves. The mother insisted that he sing.

The doctor suggested each one should play a rhythm on his instrument. I began, then the father, but when the mother did it she did not respect the rhythm of the others and she seemed to be alone.

M. identified himself with his father's beat. After a while, the mother stopped and we all followed her. Then we started again, and M. participated in the group. The mother sang "Rice Pudding,"* and the whole group accompanied her on their instruments.

I suggested we make a ring. M. was observed to drag his feet. I beat the step louder, and they all followed me and M. started walking better.

Then, I took the claves and beat the rhythm; each member of the group moved freely. I asked M. to come close to one of the walls where he would find the hoops. M. followed my indications and gave a hoop to each one of us. I threw mine on the floor, and the father asked, "Shall we play houses?" M. immediately stood in a hoop. We again played houses, which M. enjoyed

---

Translator's note: "Rice Pudding" is a nursery rhyme all Argentine children know.

very much. At one point, M. went to the father's hoop to stand in it. The father told him "...when you come in, I'll leave my house and stay outside." M. did not want his father to leave the hoop and tried to cling to him. Then he went to look for the mother's hoop. She was waiting for him anxiously.

In the meantime, I was making sounds with my hands and feet, following all the movements. Then, the mother spontaneously organized the little train and placed herself at the head, going faster and faster. M. became more and more excited. The father did not join the game until the doctor made a sign for him to do so. In this way, M. was placed between his father and his mother. They played for a while like this, accelerating and slowing down the march of the train.

The mother asked M., "...Where are we going?... to the North Pole or to the South Pole?" When the train reached a station, the mother asked, "Is it hot or cold?" Finally we sang the goodbye song and we left.

Among the comments, it was interesting to note that the mother thought that M. had enjoyed himself at this session; but the conclusion was reached that for the mother, to enjoy himself meant for M. to be excited.

The father thought that something similar occurred at home to what had happened during the session, i.e. when he spoke to M. and later did not answer him, the mother or the grandmother always intervened; this hindered communication with the father, which was rather poor as it was. The mother's difficulty was to wait until M. answered.

Third Family Group Session

During the third session, the mother came alone and explained that the father could not come to the sessions because of his work. For a year it was impossible to get the father to come.

After several meetings of the team, it was decided to hold a few sessions with the mother and the maternal grandmother, who lived with them and who was the main relation M. had.

The sessions with the grandmother were very successful, as it was possible to see many aspects of M.'s behavior that could be changed when the grandmother's attitude was changed not only towards him but also to his mother. I shall only transcribe the first session with the grandmother.

The grandmother was a central character in the family, who had taken charge of M. from the beginning. She was a strong woman, affable and consistent, wore slacks and masculine shoes.

As soon as M. entered the blue room, he went up to his grandmother and reacted with pleasure, saying "Granny!" The grandmother answered, "...are you pleased... yes, it's me."

M. was excited, rocking himself and jumping constantly. The grandmother immediately asked, "Who else is here?" M. went running to touch his mother and said "Mummy" while he went on jumping.

M. began his stereotyped game of doctors, i.e. he pricked his leg with a finger and spoke of the doctor who gave him the injections in the third person.

The grandmother was silent.

The doctor asked him, "What do you want to do, M.?

Immediately the mother intervened, saying "let's sing." The doctor answered her, "Why don't we ask M. what he wants to do?" Then the mother said to M., "What do you want to play?... Anything you like, except doctors..." M. answered, "are you going to play at doctors?..." The mother answered "No" and commented that yesterday he had begun to float in the swimming pool and that she had told him how pleased she was.

In the meantime, M. continued his stereotyped game of pricking himself as if he were giving himself an injection. This attitude was characteristic of his psychotherapy sessions where, by means of this game, he acted out the traumatic situations he had lived through when he went through numerous eye operations.

I began to sing: "walking, walking..." This stimulated the mother to get up and M. clung to her. We suggested that they should both walk separately, but the mother did not understand the instructions and did not let him go.

The grandmother made signs to her daughter to leave M. alone while she remained seated in the same place all during the session. On understanding, the mother let him go, but in spite of this, M. continued clinging to her and walked as if he were dragged.

Then I tried walking with him, but he also clung to me and let himself be dragged.

Finally, when I stopped singing, M. threw himself on the floor and began a spontaneous game, saying "I'm drowning... I'm drowning... glu, glu, glu..."

He stood up and said, "that's that..." All this was accompanied by his mother, who followed his game.

Then M. began speaking about a neurologist who attended him. I explained to him that we were not in the that doctor's office. Then M. said, "... we're in the blue room."

I asked him: Who is with us?

M.: Mummy and Granny...

I: Who else?

M.: Daddy.

I: Look for him.

M. went to where Rolando was, touched him and said, "Daddy."

I: I don't think that's Daddy.

M. touched him again and said, "Rolando."

Finally we played some instruments, beating them, and observed that M. was becoming progressively more anxious. I asked what the matter was, and he was able to say "I don't want any more..." He became quiet then, said goodbye to everybody, and returned to the classroom.

Final Conclusions

Music therapy treatment enabled M. to relive, modify, and improve his relations with his mother and his grandmother. He was able to clarify his body identity patterns. The integration of the family group enabled each member of the family to change the structure of their behavior towards M. They were able to observe the pathological communication cysts that caused the formation of bizarre behavior in M.

In spite of attending only two sessions, the father also benefited from this technique as, when he gradually received the messages from the mother and the grandmother, he also changed and achieved a better relationship with M.

During the continuous meetings of the team, especially the psychologist and the assistants at the Institute, we were able to help each other mutually to change our own behavior patterns and, above all, to brace ourselves against disappointments.

BIBLIOGRAPHY

Benenzon, Rolando: *Musicoterapia y Educación*. Buenos Aires PAIDOS, 1971.

Benenzon, Rolando and Yepes, Antonio: *Musicoterapia en Psiquiatría (metodología y Técnica)*. Buenos Aires, BARRY, 1972.

Carmichael, L.: *Manual de Psicología Infantil*. Buenos Aires, El Ateneo, 1957.

Kanner, Leo: *Psiquiatría Infantil*. Buenos Aires, PAIDOS, 1966.

Mahler, Margaret: *Simbiosis Humana: Las Vicisitudes de la Individuación*. Mexico, Joaquin Mortiz, 1972.

Rascovsky, Arnaldo: *El Psiquismo Fetal*. Buenos Aires, PAIDOS, 1960.

Rimland, B.: *Infantile Autism*. New York, Appleton-Century-Crofts, 1964.

Rodrigué, Emilio: Aporte al problema del autismo. *Revista Argentina de Psiquiatria y Psicología de la Infancia y de la Adolescencia*, Buenos Aires, 1970.

Sontag, Lester W.: Efecto del ruido durante el período del embarazo sobre el feto y la conducta adulta subsiguiente. *Revista Argentina de Psiquiatria y Psicología de la Infancia y de la Adolescencia*, ASAPPIA, Año 1, n° ¾, 1970.

INDEX

A

Amniotic liquid, 33
Anhyrridia, 69
Aphasia, 20
Autistic child, 10, 11, 20, 21, 26, 27, 39, 49, 60, 82

B

Behavior disorders, 69
Blind, 25, 61, 69, 73, 87
Braille, 81
Brain damage, 66

C

Characteropathic sound, 18
Child psychosis, 14
Clap, 68
Clicks, 41, 43
Communication channels, 1, 13, 29, 31, 45, 46, 47, 68, 75
Communication cysts, 45, 47, 54, 68, 77, 94
Communication disorders, 20
Communication level, 29, 30, 39
Continuous sound, 17
Cymbals, 59

D

Deafness, 14, 25, 48, 54, 61
Dislexias, 16
Drumstick, 66, 67, 68

E

Echolalia, 75, 87
Electronic sounds, 17, 18, 19

F

Family group, 29, 45, 57, 62, 64, 86
Family therapy, 52, 62
Fetal psyche, 14, 32
Flute, 43, 59, 68, 80, 88
Free improvisation, 4

G

Games, 25, 89
Glaucoma, 69
Group music therapy sessions, 67
Guttural sounds, 68

H

Hallucinations, 11, 18, 26
Harmonica, 80
Heart beats, 1, 15, 16, 32, 36, 42, 43
Hydrotherapy, 24
Hyperactive children, 14
Hyperkinetic fetuses, 14
Hypochondriac patients, 18

I

Integration level, 29
Intermediary object, 2, 7, 8, 30, 33, 38, 43, 58, 72, 76
Interpretations, 60
Intestinal sounds, 32
ISO, 4, 7, 32, 41, 45, 46, 65, 68, 72
    complementary, 3, 7
    gestalt, 7
    group, 7, 8
    principle, 7, 18

L

Lullaby, 50, 51, 71

M

Marital therapy, 62
Messages, 46, 50, 52, 54, 61, 84

Metamessages, 46
Mother-child relationship, 4, 5
Music therapist training personality, 2, 3, 4
Music therapist's unconscious nuclei, 4
Music therapy definition, 1
Music therapy questionnaire, 9, 32, 69, 70
Music therapy session, 34, 65, 76
Musical prejudice, 18
Muteness, 25, 27

N
Nanny, 46
Nonverbal context, 32, 61, 69, 72
Nonverbal elements, 2
Nonverbal form, 3

O
Occupational therapy, 13
Orff instruments, 59

P
Passive music therapy, 29
Patellar reflex, 18
Percussion instruments, 59
Piano, 74, 76, 80
Preverbal level, 3
Primitive sounds, 32
Psychodrama, 17
Psychotherapeutic treatment, 70
Psychotic children, 16, 32, 45
Puppet, 8

R
Regressive level, 29, 30, 39

Regressive nuclei, 2
Regressive sensations, 17
Regressive states, 1, 2, 29

S
Schizophrenic children, 11, 13, 39, 41, 49, 82
Siblings, 46, 49
Sinusoidal sounds, 1, 17, 36, 39, 40, 41, 43
Sounds
    empirical, 32
    identity, 8
    of breathing, 16, 32, 36, 42, 43
Stereotyped communication, 45
Stereotyped symptoms, 60
Surrogate mother, 34, 37, 48, 62, 63
Symbiotic child, 12
Symbolic expression, 25

T
Tambourine, 66, 67, 68
Testing, 72
Therapeutic couple, 59, 61, 62, 63
Therapeutic process, 4

U
Unconscious mechanisms, 60

W
Water, 32, 33, 82
Water drops, 37
White sound, 17